WHAT OTHERS AR
PREACHING A DISTURBING GOSPEL

This is a remarkable book. Julie Slous has combined a careful historian's eye, an ear for compelling and artful preaching, and a heart for a gospel that can often be disturbing, and she has created out of them a challenging call to a kind of preaching that does more than soothe hearers. She transforms her deep appreciation for the legacy of Salvation Army preaching into a very practical set of methods for preachers who wish to extend that tradition into today's context.

—*Thomas G. Long, Bandy Professor of Preaching,*
   Candler School of Theology, Atlanta, GA

Preaching a Disturbing Gospel by Julie Slous is a must-read for anyone who desires to preach with intensity and fire. Written in a straightforward, thought-provoking style, this volume is both a fascinating, comprehensive historic record, as well as a refreshing, practical how-to manual on the art and power of preaching. I highly recommend this informative, inspirational and challenging book.

—*Commissioner William W. Francis, Chairman,*
   The Salvation Army International Doctrine Council

Julie Slous is a splendid preacher and teacher who is concerned about listeners' needs in the postmodern world. Situating Salvationist preaching in its historical and social context, she advocates providing an experience of the gospel over explanation, and offers three excellent strategies for achieving that goal: orientation, disorientation and reorientation. Preachers from any background could benefit from her guidance.

—*Paul Scott Wilson, Professor of Homiletics,*
  Emmanuel College, University of Toronto

Julie Slous' objective is to teach preachers to disturb their hearers—because that is the intention of the Bible. The Good News is transformative news. Those who hear it are to be changed by it. The theory of this book has been honed by real preaching to real people. I am one of those people. As my corps officer, Julie Slous has been my preacher for five years, and I am the better for it.

—*James E. Read, PhD, Executive Director, The Salvation Army*
  Ethics Centre, Corps Sergeant-Major, Heritage Park Temple

PREACHING A DISTURBING GOSPEL

JULIE A. SLOUS
FOREWORD **ROGER J. GREEN**

Published by The Salvation Army, Canada and Bermuda Territory
2 Overlea Blvd., Toronto, Ontario M4H 1P4
Phone: 416.422.6110 Fax: 416.422.6120
www.salvationarmy.ca

Cover Design: Brandon Laird
Cover Photos: 1. Zsolt Biczó; 2. Carson Samson; 3. Olga Yakovenko;
4. http://www.flickr.com/photos/victoriapeckham;
Layout and Design: Brandon Laird

Printed in Canada
ISBN: 978-0-88857-500-5

The assistance of these contributors in preparing this book is greatly
appreciated:

Major Fred Ash, members of the Territorial Literature Council, staff of
the Editorial Department (Editor-in-Chief and Literary Secretary:
Major Jim Champ)

TABLE OF CONTENTS

FOREWORD

THE FOUNDERS OF THE SALVATION ARMY SHOULD BE remembered primarily as preachers, and this work is constructed on that basic truth. Preaching the gospel message to the masses was the main task of both William and Catherine Booth throughout their lives. Their heroes in the Christian faith, whether living or dead, were preachers—John Wesley, James Caughey and Charles Grandison Finney to name a few. It is little wonder that when the Booths founded The Christian Mission the buildings were called Preaching Stations. Christian Missioners were expected relentlessly to preach the gospel in the meeting places and on the streets, and their preaching resulted in the salvation of sinners and the raising up of saints. The preached Word was the fire that lit up The Christian Mission and later The Salvation Army.

The Booths, both of whom were nurtured in Wesleyan Methodism, knew that in the Protestant tradition the indispensible sign of the Christian Church is preaching. All who had been faithful to that duty, from Martin Luther to Charles Spurgeon, called generations of listeners to the glorious gospel of Christ. The Booths were committed to that task and expected others around them to be likewise faithful.

The legacy of the Booths is their explicit recognition of the gospel as both good news and hard news in every context and culture, and preaching only one or the other does no justice to the whole written Word. Julie Slous strikes a graceful balance between the two, even for a contemporary generation that finds the words of the preacher out of touch with the present cultural discourse. She also faces the reality of a different contemporary world from the world of the Booths. The authority of the preacher in this age is not a given as it was in Victorian England. Every preacher will do well to understand this without being discouraged by it.

This work reminds us that only the preacher who seeks truth rather than relevance will realize the power of the preached Word. For that reason and many others this book should be read by everyone compelled to preach the gospel of Christ and his kingdom.

Roger J. Green, PhD, D.D., O.F.
Professor and Chair of Biblical Studies and Christian Ministries
Terrelle B. Crum Chair of Humanities
Gordon College
Wenham, MA

PREFACE

JOHN WESLEY WAS ONCE ASKED WHY SO MANY PEOPLE CAME to hear him preach. His response was, "When you set yourself on fire, people love to come and see you burn."[1] While the question pushed to understand why the masses were so intrigued with Wesley's pulpit, we might well ask today, what is really happening in our pulpits to capture the interest and the attention of today's listener? If we were to survey local congregations, perhaps we would be surprised to learn how many people would like to see a little more fire burning in the pulpit on a Sunday morning! It presses us to ask what preaching is accomplishing in today's contemporary world. Is preaching waking people up or is it painfully lulling them to sleep? Is preaching inspiring, motivating and reaching people where they are, or has the relevancy of this time-honoured tradition within the Christian Church lost esteem and effectiveness?

Using these initial questions as a launching pad, the pages that follow seek to put the reality of the contemporary pulpit in conversation with a place in history where homiletical fires burned with notable intensity. Drawing from the richness of The Salvation Army's story, we reach back into the Victorian and Edwardian eras (1819-1930) to encounter the aggressive proclamation of a disturbing gospel. We do not have to travel far to recognize this as a form of confrontational preaching that took society by storm. It was within this setting that the preaching ministry of The Salvation Army entered the ecumenical arena in 1865. The primary evangelistic voices of the Movement belonged to its first leaders and preachers, William and Catherine Booth. Motivated by the scope of human suffering that was present in the East End of London, England, the Booths responded where no other agency or transforming influence was present. They stepped into a societal gap to bring good news to the poor. They believed in the importance of preaching a disturbing gospel; that which would represent the hard claims of the gospel, requiring listeners to pay attention to the deep eternal truths of God. The mandate was to preach about that which really mattered: "At the time of eternal reckoning, sinner will your life be right with God?"

As we encounter the very aggressive nature of early Salvation Army preaching, it becomes clear that pulpit fires were burning fiercely throughout Victorian England. The emphasis given to preaching the hard claims of the gospel is unavoidably central to what is observed. We ask whether there is any relevance in this approach for today. Is there still a place for confrontational preaching in the contemporary pulpit? Does this approach to preaching help to address some of the very real challenges we are facing in engaging today's listener?

In attempting to assess that which we encounter in the early tradition of Salvation Army preaching, we acknowledge the sensitivity of the human spirit toward the harsh themes of God's judgment, wrath and eternal damnation. We search for ways to proclaim faithfully all of God's truth, while effectively engaging our audience. Will we avoid difficult, weighted messages just because these make people uncomfortable? How will we help people to hear the news that they are fallen creatures, "totally depraved, and as such are justly exposed to the wrath of God"[2]? In our present day context, we acknowledge that secular society has become distant to the language of sin and judgment. How will we encourage people to see their need for a Saviour, or ultimately suffer the eternal consequences of sin? In many respects, it has become easier to ignore this conversation rather than risk relationally alienating people by this disturbing claim. This has become an increasing tension as contemporary society has sought to become more sensitive and tolerant toward ethnic and religious diversity.

With this foundation established, the stated tensions are compounded further by my own personal experience. Having sat in the vantage point of the pew, I have become acutely aware of what it is like to leave the preaching event unaffected and questioning the point of my time spent listening. Perhaps there are readers that can identify! Conversely, this is placed alongside experiences where preaching has been stimulating and life-changing. Recognizing the disparity between these two realities, this book asks what help is available to the preacher to offer a more engaging word to today's congregants. What influence might renewed aggression and energy have in achieving this goal as today's preacher considers what it looks like to proclaim a disturbing gospel?

Within the chapters that follow, readers will discover that cited quotations will not demonstrate gender inclusivity. The intent to capture and maintain historical accuracy has remained central to this project, while seeking to navigate with faithfulness and academic integrity the patriarchal era out of which the early Salvation Army emerged. Readers will also note that all Scripture references are from the New International Version.

As the fiery embers of the past extend their flame toward the challenges of the present, this journey is fueled by a hope that new conversations will emerge about preaching, both in Salvation Army circles and beyond. How can today's preachers realistically address the challenges of the days in which they live? Readers are invited to hold the principles discussed in this book alongside that which they see represented before them on a Sunday morning. What do we see happening in our contemporary pulpits? Why might people come to hear preaching? What is being disturbed and ultimately what is changing because of the faithful proclamation of God's Word? Can the preacher's message find new relevance for today's world?

Born out of a deep conviction that renewal in contemporary preaching can come through renewed emphasis toward the disturbing claims of the gospel, we lean back into the past and listen to those who have travelled this road before us. Ironically, we will discover some of the same challenges that confronted the first preachers of The Salvation Army are still our challenges today. Toward these tensions, our attention is turned.

ACKNOWLEDGMENTS

THERE ARE MANY WHO SHARE IN THE MILESTONE OF THIS work coming to fruition. To former preaching professors John Rottman and Paul Wilson; appreciation is given for the manner in which you inspired a deeper investigation of a new form of homiletic in this preacher's life. That which initially sparked within your classrooms has grown into a blazing fire.

To students of The College for Officer Training in Toronto, St. John's and Winnipeg, Canada, who for the past fourteen years have not only stimulated but probed my thinking to address the deeper issues of Salvation Army preaching; your fingerprints are all over this manuscript.

To the congregation of Heritage Park Temple, Winnipeg, which allowed me Sunday after Sunday to put theory into practice; your eagerness for God's Word has spurred me toward trying to say something that might make a difference in the landscape of our times.

To thesis advisor Dr. Richard Rehfeldt and colleagues of my Luther Cohort; your questions have pressed me to greater depths. The richness of our learning together has been an invaluable part of this journey as we have brought together the diversity of all our preaching traditions.

To The Salvation Army Canada and Bermuda Territory and in particular the territorial executive leadership team; your support provided both the means and the opportunity for this research to find its footing. Subsequently, you have opened the way for this work to extend its impact beyond that of its original audience. May there be continued confirmation of the worth of this investment. Special thanks are also offered to Major Fred Ash whose keen editorial wit and flair for the written word have been a great source of inspiration toward the preparation of these pages for publication.

Finally and most importantly to my husband Brian and our children Jennifer, Jonathan and Brittany—thank you for allowing our lives to be disturbed while this work was completed. Your unending love, support and encouragement have meant so much as this chapter of our lives has been written.

INTRODUCTION

"There is no improving the future, without disturbing the present and the difficulty is to get people to be willing to be disturbed!"
—Catherine Booth, 1880[1]

WHEN CATHERINE BOOTH (1829-1890), CO-FOUNDER of The Salvation Army, first uttered these words, there was a clear view of the kingdom of God at hand. Catherine believed in preaching a "disturbing gospel" wherein which the harsh themes of judgment, God's wrath, eternal separation and spiritual indifference could not be ignored by the preacher. This was essential in seeking to represent the full counsel of God. Catherine Booth quickly discerned the complacency of the society in which she lived. There was too much "settledness" toward sin. In order for the future to become better than the present, slumbering sinners needed to be disturbed; they needed to be awakened to the transforming power of the Word of God and the significance of a personal experience of salvation. The weight of Catherine's convictions hammered their way into her 1883 sermon, entitled *Religious Indifference*. The following excerpt not only arrested the attention of the original audience but now, crossing a great historical divide, demands a hearing in our time and space:

> Satan has got men fast asleep in sin and that it is his great device to keep them so.... We may sing songs about the sweet by-and-by, preach sermons, say prayers, and go the jog-trot round and round, barrel-organ fashion, till Doomsday, and he will never concern himself about us if we don't wake anybody up.... That is your responsibility you Christians.... Wake him! WAKE HIM! Remember, sinners are indifferent.[2]

In today's world, themes of political correctness, gender inclusion and accommodation for ethnic diversity dominate theological discussion. In light of these perceived sensitivities, does an aggressive confrontational approach to preaching have a place in current thought? What is the contemporary preacher to do with the *disturbing* message of the gospel? The Apostle Paul does not hold back any ammunition when he says: "There is no one righteous, not even one... all have sinned and fall short of the glory of God" (Romans 3:10, 23). Let the obvious be stated. The preacher has a tough job! Motivated by the compelling love of Christ, the task is to show a complacent world how it is out of step with God. The supreme task of preaching is to awaken the slumbering consciousness of the sinner; to point out the eternal hopelessness of the sinful condition and to challenge a turning toward God through confession and repentance of heart. It is a difficult message, and one that is not easily heard. It calls for a depth of human introspection and honesty—perhaps, most significantly, it requires a surrender of the will to God. This can seem an extremely troubling and even offensive message to those who are convinced that they have no need of a Saviour. How aggressively should the preacher therefore proclaim, "Now is the time of God's favour, now is the day of salvation" (2 Corinthians 6:2)? How earnestly does the preacher seek to disturb the settled nature of the sinful heart for the purpose of enlivening it toward the abundance of God's grace and love? How forcefully does the preacher pursue this task before distancing the listener completely from the good news that is delivered?

The tension articulated is not a new conversation to the discipline of preaching. For centuries preachers have sought to work out the delicate balance between the proclamation of law and grace; the bad news versus the good news. Volumes line our shelves speaking to this reality. The debate, however, intensifies in contemporary context where so much time and effort is applied to inclusive/seeker- sensitive worship. The primary emphasis is that the gospel should not seem too pushy and that people could seek after faith in a non-threatening environment. If this is our approach, is it possible that we may water down the gospel message for fear that its power and potency will simply overwhelm and alienate our listeners? Does the gospel end up losing the spotlight it deserves? Do we maintain integrity in biblical preaching by this way of thinking?

The preaching tradition of The Salvation Army finds a unique place in this debate and has much to offer in resolving the stated tensions. Born out of the spirit of revivalism in 1865, this evangelical Movement founded by William Booth (1829-1912) and his wife, Catherine Booth (1829-1890), became an aggressive homiletical presence in Victorian England. When the Booths recognized the difference a "disturbing gospel" could make to their societal context, their preaching ministry took flight. Fueled by the depravity and destitution of those who lived in the slums of East End London, this early form of Salvation Army preaching grounded itself on strong convictions. They believed without reservation in the possible conversion of the heathen masses to Christianity, and that this alone could transform the landscape of the times in which the people lived.[3] In order to achieve this goal, the necessity of opposing the staid complacency of both Christians and non-believers alike was critical. The early Salvationist[4] was therefore encouraged to be "God's Great Disturber of the Peace" forcing men and women to think of God and his claims upon their lives. Salvationists were encouraged to turn the world upside down—to overthrow the Devil—to annihilate selfishness—to make all things new.[5] People required some kind of warning to alert them of their need for salvation. The means to achieve this came through untiring, uncompromising agitation.

> The early Salvationist was therefore encouraged to be "God's Great Disturber of the Peace" forcing men and women to think of God and his claims upon their lives

While today's preacher must blow the dust off the historical manuscripts containing these emphases, a preaching philosophy emerges that demands a hearing. This system of early Salvation Army preaching rises from the shadows of the past and pleads its relevance for today. To the preacher longing that preaching might achieve renewed power and vitality in the pulpit, this approach to proclamation invites exploration. Those who set out on this journey, however, are duly warned. An overwhelming sense of urgency and passion will confront us. This form of preaching will not entertain debate about political correctness or seeker sensitivity. Rather, those representing this approach to preaching will speak only in absolutes. Sinners are in need of salvation. Jesus Christ is the only way to eternal life. We will be reminded how humanity has always lived de-sensitized to its deep spiritual need. Those crossing this great historical divide will wrestle with the appropriate manner in which a preacher seeks to wake up sleeping sinners and how this is best achieved. The issues confronting us are credibility versus manipulation; authenticity versus exploitation; grace versus judgment; and most importantly the supremacy of unconditional love versus a reality of unrelenting condemnation.

Those who sign on for this exploratory journey recognize that their ultimate destination is to get inside this early form of Salvation Army preaching. Key questions provide a sense of direction:

1. What defines the early Salvationist/Booth style of preaching?

2. What fueled Salvation Army preaching beyond the Movement's formative years?

3. What philosophical and theological principles lie beneath the proclamation of this gospel intended to "disturb" sinners' consciousness and awaken them to eternal life?

4. How does the preaching legacy of William and Catherine Booth assist today's preacher in re-contextualizing what the proclamation of a "disturbing" gospel can look like in a contemporary setting?

In order to probe these significant areas of discussion, specific voices must enter into this conversation, beginning with the Founders themselves. Chapter 1 will therefore focus on an exploration of the distinct homiletic (or preaching style) of William and Catherine Booth.[6] What defined and influenced their earliest expression of biblical preaching? Consideration will be given to both external and internal factors, for it quickly becomes apparent that a multiplicity of personalities and experiences contributed to the homiletical "DNA" represented. In many respects, William and Catherine became the trendsetters for what subsequently took place in Salvation Army pulpits. Through their distinct confrontational style of preaching, they provided a template for those who followed. In studying this homiletical period in history, it becomes evident that a specific preaching legacy is handed down to Salvationists through the Booths. Understanding the substance and design of this is critical to discerning the essence of early Salvation Army preaching.

Chapter 2 will give a more detailed assessment of what fueled this early Salvation Army/Booth homiletic beyond the Movement's formative years. In this respect, the primary questions become, "What kept the Booths' style of preaching alive?" "What ensured its advancement?" "What foundational convictions contributed to an emerging theology of preaching?" The intrinsic relationship of preaching to Salvation Army mission will become an unavoidable conversation partner in this discussion. This will lead to a synthesis of historical findings through which we might more specifically define the legacy inherited by the contemporary preacher. Evidence will point toward a homiletic based upon the proclamation of a *disturbing gospel,* meaning that the intention of preaching is to break up the settled nature of the human mind and will, exposing it to the transforming power of God's love revealed through Jesus Christ and nurtured through the Holy Spirit.

Using earlier chapters as a backdrop, Chapter 3 will invite readers to take a journey toward the lived realities of 19th-century Victorian England. As early Salvationist preachers heralded the bold claims of the gospel into this context, we ask why Victorian audiences seemed so warmly disposed to what they were hearing and receiving. Crossing this historical divide, we will find significant markers to navigate including a strong sense of social respectability that emerges through religious observance. The manner in which this shaped Victorian belief systems and behaviour is profound. The ground upon which we walk in these pages will demonstrate the favourable conditions into which a *disturbing gospel* first went as William and

Catherine Booth sought to be faithful to God's calling and purposes for their lives.

Chapter 4 will invite contrast and comparison as readers open a place to identify what is defining of their own cultural context. How are the realities of living in a postmodern/post-Christian world similar to the realities of Victorian England? Where do we find common ground? Where do we differ? Most significantly, in this chapter we will wrestle with how we deal with the diminishing respect and regard of society for the authority of the Church, particularly as it relates to defining truth. Today's preachers must navigate these troubling waters and rediscover how they can recapture the attention of an audience that has become convinced their best answer to life's deepest question is an accommodating "whatever!" In contrasting the differences between Victorian and postmodern/post-Christian realities, a clear picture emerges as to what our challenges really are in this conversation.

Chapter 5 seeks movement toward practical application and asks if the principles found within the Booths' early approach to preaching are transferable to biblical preaching in a postmodern/post-Christian context.[7] Readers will note emphasis toward defining how the threads of postmodern thinking influence the landscape of our times. These threads weave themselves within nuances represented by an increasingly post-Christian-thinking world. In this respect, the influence of pluralistic thought and the migration of people from other religions into our societal framework have significant impact. Christianity can no longer claim its primary place as a dominant civil religion but must share the spotlight with a wide variety of worldviews and ideologies that frame varying religious movements. Eddie Gibbs, in *Church Next,* suggests that the Western world cannot understand its current ministry context without making this distinction.[8] With this foundation established, we ask what is different about the context of Victorian England versus our present cultural address. While Victorian England warmed up to the gospel, those of postmodern/post-Christian perspective cool. What significant shifts have occurred in both religious and moral norms that contribute to this reality? How does the mission field of William and Catherine Booth differ from the places where God's people serve today? While acknowledging the difficulties of rekindling the flame, this chapter also presents six principles that will aid in getting those fires restarted.

Chapter 6 will argue for an assimilation and re-contextualization of the Booths' early approach to preaching, leading us to identify what we will affectionately call a *new Salvationist homiletic*. Herein, we uncover valuable principles and priorities for today's preacher who must convince contemporary listeners that there is a reason to engage the claims of a disturbing gospel.

"In every age of Christianity, there has been no great religious movement, no restoration of Scripture truth, and reanimation of genuine piety without *new power* in preaching both as cause and effect"

Part II of this work will offer tangible resources that will lift the theory and principles of this book to a place of practical application. By inviting new ways to think about biblical texts, preachers will be encouraged to consider what becomes disorientating about Scripture. What disturbs us or unsettles us? What speed bumps do we have to navigate to get to the heart of the text's message for our time and space? Only as the preacher unlocks the energy and tension that is behind a given text, will there be a possibility for passionate proclamation. Well-focused exegetical engagement will be the secret to this process and specific strategies assist this work. Sample sermons provide examples of how exegetical ideas grow into a structure for preaching and how these ideas can take flight in a congregational setting.

As we reach conclusion, the intent of this work is that both principles and practical strategies for preaching a disturbing gospel will have met in these pages. Drawing from the richness of a homiletical legacy given to the Church from an era now quite remote from our own, we discover a means of breathing fresh life and vitality into contemporary pulpits. Strong, effective, engaging biblical preaching that seeks "to disturb the present to better the future" speaks to this possibility. John Broadus (1827-1895) reinforced this perspective when he said, "In every age of Christianity, there has been no great religious movement, no restoration of Scripture truth, and reanimation of genuine piety without *new power* [emphasis mine] in preaching both as cause and effect."[9]

Surprisingly, homiletical explorers may discover, in these pages, the source of this new power within an old homiletic once buried in Salvation Army history, yet now emerging with contemporary relevance and application. While adaptation will be necessary, its overriding principles and theological convictions will be a reminder of how proclamation of a disturbing gospel can lead to the betterment of the world in which we live. The appropriate balance between the preaching of judgment and grace will be a key component to this re-contextualization process. As this is achieved, readers will be invited to take hold of the treasure that has been uncovered and its intrinsic value for the contemporary proclamation of the gospel message.

PART I

THE DISTURBING GOSPEL

CHAPTER 1

RED-HOT PREACHING

His [William Booth's] gospel has been a wide one; it has covered the sins and sorrows and wounds of all mankind; he has preached of God the Father, God the Son and God the Holy Ghost with the result that I have seen tears flow, heads bowed, lips quiver, hearts broken, rebels reconciled, prodigals come home, wanderers return, and sinners of all classes reconciled to God.[1]

... but within five minutes she [Catherine Booth] had captured the attention of all the group, and in five minutes more had made a way to their hearts.... Again and again, at the close of an address, I have heard men of widely differing classes exclaim with conviction, 'O my God, I never thought I was like that—what shall I do? What shall I do?'[2]

TEPPING BACK INTO THE EARLY DAYS OF THE SALVATION Army, we are confronted with a powerful and inspiring reality—Salvation Army preaching had impact! Evidence pours forth as to how Salvation Army preaching connected biblical truths with the desperate plight of suffering humanity and miraculously motivated a movement toward repentance and faith. Preaching aimed for results. Preaching achieved results! Early testimonials overflow with Spirit-filled evidence of the powerful way in which the Word of God was reaching human hearts.

After preaching a short time the influence increased and
the power of God came down on the people, and there
was such shouting and weeping that I [Catherine Booth]
was compelled to break it off and invite the wounded to
come forward. Many responded and 26 were converted.
It was a glorious season. There must have been nearly 40
seeking mercy at one time.[3]

So great was the number of penitents that Mr. Booth had
the usual communion rails extended right across the entire
breadth of the chapel, besides erecting barriers to keep
off the crowds of onlookers, who pressed so closely to the
front that it was found impossible to deal effectually with
those who were seeking salvation.[4]

Such stories stir the human spirit! They speak to the possibility
that Pentecost could come once again to the Church; that flames of
living fire could fall upon us in fresh ways, inspiring renewed
response and commitment to the Christian faith. If it happened in
the past, surely it is possible again here in the present! We ask, practically, what contributed to these remarkable testimonials? What
approach to preaching did the early Salvationist use to facilitate
these incredible results? How does the strategy and methodology we
observe contribute to our understanding of that which becomes a
unique and distinct Salvation Army homiletic?

In order to answer this question, it is necessary to shine an investigative light into the past. The first form of a Salvation Army homiletic
emerged in the ministry of William and Catherine Booth, and from
them a model for biblical preaching was initially established. As a systematic inquiry is made of historical sources, we recognize this
homiletic (or this form of preaching) was not shaped within a formal
academic arena. William and Catherine did not have the benefit of
seminary training or focused instruction that taught them how to be
effective expositors of Holy Scripture, like many preachers today.[5] An
understanding of early Salvation Army preaching therefore begins by
extracting from history that which assisted in shaping the practice of
biblical preaching for William and Catherine Booth.

The Glory of a Personal Conversion Experience

In many respects, this is an obvious point of beginning. The words of the preacher cannot be formed in the mind and articulated by the mouth, until there is an experience of Christ in the heart. Norman H. Murdoch, in his work *Origins of The Salvation Army*, suggests that both William and Catherine had difficulty citing their exact moment of conversion. Perhaps not all scholars would agree with this position,[6] yet we are able to see a picture of a progressive faith journey, as we piece together varying historical sources. Multiple events, circumstances and influences would seem to have contributed to the overall way in which God was working and moving in the lives of the Booths, preparing them for their life's calling.

The family background of both William and Catherine is a necessary and helpful backdrop to this discussion. Catherine's upbringing had been very religious, being raised under the puritanical rule of her mother, who required her to read from the Bible as early as age three. Consequently, she had actually read the Bible eight times in its entirety by age 12.[7] What a notable accomplishment, given that many people today cannot boast of having read the Bible through even once!

William's story was different. His childhood had been very unhappy. He was born into a substantial middle-class family that fell upon desperate times because of his father's materialistic preoccupations, which ultimately led to the family's financial ruin. William described his father as one who knew no greater gain or end than money.[8] In his own testimony regarding this period of his life, a window is opened to see not only the desperate nature of the times, but also the deep affection he carried for his mother. She was a woman who, in William's estimation, could have died of a broken heart, yet she continually "upheld his father's spirit as crash after crash followed and one piece of property after another went overboard." Knowing this firsthand experience of economic misfortune, William understood what it meant to live among the poorer classes; those who were being reduced to the verge of starvation.[9]

With this background established, both William and Catherine gave witness to a time of "spiritual crises" in their teenage years. This led to a deep awareness of sin and an intense yearning after

God. Murdoch claims this turning point for William was primarily due to his father's death; Catherine's resulted from her father's turning from a narrow path of Wesleyan temperance to alcoholism.[10] Elaborating upon this further, Roger Green in *Catherine Booth* offers a detailed description of William's spiritual pilgrimage, highlighting his initial religious learning, primarily due to the influence of his mother. Adding to this, William found his Wesleyan footing within services at the Broad Street Wesleyan Methodist Chapel. An elderly couple who were friends of the family ensured that he attended regularly. While William considered himself a nominal Christian in these earlier years, the records suggest in 1844, at age 15, he was fully converted under the influence of preacher Isaac Marsden.[11]

The preaching that William encountered contributed to a *stirring of the spirit,* which urged him toward a more public declaration of faith and commitment. His attendance at the Wesleyan Class Meetings intensified this state of conviction, especially when he was called upon to represent the state of his soul. While such a tactic today might seem imposing, for William having to answer to his spiritual condition became a formative moment in his faith journey. This is where the famous story of the silver pencil case comes into the picture.[12] Apparently, during a boyish trading affair, William had made a profit while leading his friends to believe that he had done them a favour. As an expression of their appreciation, they gave him a silver pencil case. According to biographer Harold Begbie, William struggled with this unresolved sin and it ultimately inhibited an act of public surrender. In William's own words, we see the depth of struggle that was represented: "The inward Light revealed to me ... that I must not only renounce everything I knew to be sinful, but make restitution, so far as I had the ability, for any wrong I had done to others before I could find peace with God.[13] Begbie suggests that this "silver pencil case burned like fire against flesh."[14] Restitution with his peers was necessary if William was going to have any sense of spiritual resolve. Finding the young fellow he had wronged, William returned the undeserved pencil case, and gave witness to "the instant rolling away from [his] heart of the guilty burden, the peace that came in its place, and the going forth to serve God and [his] generation from that hour."[15]

Conversely, Catherine reported being "truly and savingly converted at the age of 16."[16] What then can be made of the intensity of religious instruction that Catherine knew in her upbringing? Was this all without impact or effect? Given Catherine's analytical disposition, it could be argued that her struggle was to resolve a tension between the rational and the experiential nature of her faith. How was one to know the true assurance of salvation and Christ's indwelling? Roger Green further represents this great controversy of Catherine's soul, reflecting that she had lived a blameless life as far as outward experience was concerned. She had a passionate zeal for the gospel and gladly used the means of grace provided by the Church. Yet she still found herself consumed with personal doubts and often struggled with an angry temper. How would she find the assurance that she truly was a child of God?[17]

Catherine's moment of spiritual breakthrough came early one morning as she lay in bed reflecting on these words from one of Charles Wesley's hymns: "My God I am Thine, What a comfort Divine, What a blessing to know that my Jesus is mine!" Roger Green further relates the account drawing from the historical perspective of W.T. Stead's *Mrs. Booth of The Salvation Army*:

> Scores of times I had read and sung these words, but now they came to my inmost soul with a force and illumination they had never before possessed. It was as impossible for me to doubt as it would have been before for me to exercise faith. Previously not all the promises in the Bible could induce me to believe: now not all the devils in hell could persuade me to doubt. I no longer hoped that I was saved, I was certain of it. The assurances of my salvation seemed to flood and fill my soul. I jumped out of bed, and without waiting to dress, ran into my mother's room and

told her what had happened.[18]

Now fully convinced of salvation and assured of personal victory from sin, the way was prepared for both William and Catherine to join their stories together for the ultimate purpose of doing the will of God.[19] Yet the way forward would not be without significant challenges and obstacles. Moments of doubt would still come but what remained constant was a clear understanding of a full experience of Christ. Theirs was a personal salvation. William and Catherine had experienced the transformation that came with the blessing of a clean heart. *This enabled the Booths to become first-hand witnesses to the gospel they would later proclaim.* Such an example surfaces in the sampling of a sermon Catherine delivered in the summer of 1880, during a series of services in the West End of London:

> We Christians profess to possess in the gospel of Christ a mighty lever which, rightly and universally applied, would lift the entire burden of sin and misery from the shoulders, that is, from the souls, of our fellow men—a panacea, we believe it to be, for all the moral and spiritual woes of humanity.[20]

Catherine could make this claim with such confidence because she knew it to be true within her own life. Similarly, the experiential convictions of William would find their way into his messages, as demonstrated in this excerpt from *The Officer* magazine in 1893:[21]

> For an officer to speak effectively of the things of God he must be soundly converted, and either have experienced the blessing of perfect love or be on full stretch to find it, and have been baptized after Pentecostal fashion with an all-consuming love of God and souls. He should know these things, seeing that they must constitute the chief theme of his preaching, and officers should *mix up their own testimony* [emphasis mine] with their explanations and exhortations.[22]

Reinforcement of this theme finds a later expression within *The*

War Cry, 1912, warning officer-preachers against overloading their speaking with doctrinal contentions. "The chief arsenal is experience. He never wearies in attesting in one form or another, 'I know in whom I have believed' " (2 Timothy 1:12b).[23] Such becomes the strength and power of this early homiletic (or system of preaching), first defined by William and Catherine Booth. Experience could echo a resounding "amen" proclaiming that this gospel was true and trustworthy. Perhaps William expressed his most profound thoughts on this matter in his "Hints to a Preacher," published in the *East London Christian Mission* magazine in 1868:

> Preach as a dying man to a dying man.... Many will chide you and say it's all excitement; but you who have partaken of the refreshing influence of the Holy Ghost, and have tasted the good things of God, will know the reality and blessedness of this work.[24]

What then defines this early homiletic of The Salvation Army, first represented by the Booths? Clearly, something was inspired from a spiritual banquet of which both William and Catherine had partaken. Having tasted of the truth and life-changing power of the gospel, they were being prepared to become authentic representatives of this experience to others.

The Centrality of Scripture to the Preaching Task

Moving through the pages of Salvation Army history, it becomes quite evident that the centrality of Scripture not only focuses but also defines homiletical expression. The Word of God becomes the substance of truth for all preaching. William represents this emphasis particularly in his 1892 doctrinal summary prepared for educational purposes within the Training Home setting:

> The Army does solemnly and most emphatically regard the Bible as the divinely authorized standard by which all other professed revelations are to be tried, and if any professed revelation speak and square not according to

that standard, such revelations are to be rejected as having no truth in them. Whatever is contrary to the teaching of this book must be considered false, and overboard.[25]

With this emphasis affirmed, we juxtapose the concepts of biblical authority and biblical relevancy. An early Salvation Army homiletic seems to give much attention toward the latter, working aggressively to articulate the relevancy of biblical truth to practical everyday life. Recognizing the pressing need to communicate the Bible as a guide to Christian life and practice, William and Catherine Booth abandoned any kind of emphasis toward theological treatises in their preaching. The Salvationist preacher needed to get to the "heart of the matter;" the great "so what" of the homiletical process. In 1901, Bramwell Booth (son of William and Catherine) published his thoughts within *The Field Officer* magazine,[26] reinforcing the theme of his Salvationist parents. Officers were encouraged to recognize the importance of understanding Scripture in practical terms. Within this statement, we see the formation of a preaching legacy that will define a later pulpit period.

> The Salvationist preacher needed to get to the "heart of the matter;" the great "so what" of the homiletical process

We want more and more to exalt the Bible as the great guide of thought and life. Amidst the silly quibblings of a would-be-learned age; in spite of the grotesque absurdities of modern belief, and the widespread neglect of God and his wisdom which appear on every hand, we believe in the Old Book. We wish only to understand what God wants to say to us through his words; and in the strength of the Holy Ghost, to pass on to others the lessons that He teaches us. We care absolutely nothing for discussions that are merely learned.... We take up God's Book that we may know what He would have us do today.[27]

Central to the preaching task, William and Catherine Booth also understood the truth of Scripture to be the heart of what could make a difference in the life of an individual who was outside the realm of God's kingdom. The Bible made the sinner's plight uncomfortably clear. Consequently, early Salvationists were encouraged to categorize their audience by three biblical truths:

1. Sinners are taken up with the things of the world–

2. Rebels against God, and–

3. Condemned to everlasting death.[28]

In contrast to this bad news, Scripture also provided hope—the good news of the gospel of Jesus Christ. Judgment was not to have the last word in the Salvationist's approach to preaching. Rather it was critical that there be proclamation of Christ's atonement on the cross and the manner in which this finished work of salvation provided humans with a remedy to their sin problem. William reflects this emphasis further in his 1892 summary doctrinal statements.

> The sinner's great need for the truth of the gospel stands central to the preaching task

> That Christ when he died on the cross, put himself in the place of the sinner and bore the *exact amount of punishment* which he deserved, thus actually *paying the debt* that the sinner owed to divine justice. And that if the sinner will only believe this, he is for ever *free* from the claims of the law, and can never be brought into condemnation either here or hereafter.[29]

The sinner's great need for the truth of the gospel stands central to the preaching task. This gospel's source of authority came from Scripture alone, wherein the themes of law and grace came by divine authorship. With this established, the most pressing priority was to get the Bible inside the sinner. Representing the depth of this conviction, William Booth said: "We had God in man 2,000 years ago; now we need the Bible in man."[30] Early Salvationists would push the boundaries of every established norm to achieve the reality of which he spoke. The foundational philosophy driving this approach was a deeply held belief of how the Bible could be a means through which sinners could find their way out of sin's grip. William Booth captured this sentiment in a unique way when he spoke about the Bible "as a fire escape by which men could be pulled out of the raging fire of sin; a lifeboat by which they could be rescued from the stormy waves of everlasting destruction; a ladder up which they could climb to the golden gates of the City of God."[31] The truth of Scripture clearly was the means through which the sinner accessed the hope of eternal life. The early Booth homiletic pressed the priority of this element time and time again.

As this emphasis is uncovered, a tension emerges which will thread its way through this historical journey. As the early Salvationist preacher elevated the importance of relevancy within preaching; did this happen at the expense of thorough exegetical and theological development? In other words, was the substance of preaching compromised by a desire to make the Word of practical use to the listener?

William and Catherine Booth would ultimately hold to the conviction that Salvationist preachers must put within their listeners' reach that which they can grasp. If the Bible failed to be understandable, preaching failed to achieve its ultimate purpose. People would miss the message of hope offered. Historical readers can only use their best judgment to discern whether this had impact on the manner to which biblical preaching achieved depth of theological treatment.

A Distinct Calling to Cultural Context

It cannot be overstated how much the plight of human suffering had impacted the heart and mind of young William Booth. Profoundly influenced by the sights of the East End of London,

Booth saw no option but to respond to the overwhelming depravity before him. It was from this societal address, where people were living in a state of heart-wrenching despair, that William and Catherine Booth identified their first audience. The shape and design of their sermons takes flight from this point:

> He [William Booth] saw five-year-olds blind drunk at tap-room doors; mothers force feeding beer from white-chipped jugs down babies' throats. Outside pub after pub, silent savage men with ashen faces, coats piled near by, lunged and struck and toppled heavily and watching women, faces with animal passion screamed 'Strike'.... He saw children fashioning their toys from street garbage. As adults the streets were their eating place.... In the dark alleys, near the docks, the sick, the dying, often the dead, lay side by side on bare floors of fireless rooms, covered with tattered scraps of blankets. Their homes smelt of red herrings, stale bedding and last week's rain.[32]

In describing his reasons for settling in the East End of London and the scope of the social problems observed, William Booth offered the following commentary:

> In every direction, there were multitudes totally ignorant of the gospel, and given up to all kinds of wickedness— infidels, drunkards, thieves, harlots, gamblers, blasphemers and pleasure seekers without number. It was believed that out of a population of nearly a million souls that some eight hundred thousand never crossed the threshold of a church or chapel.... The strangest and the falsest notions about God, religion and the future state prevailed; and thus consequently, misery and vice were rampant everywhere. To meet and stem this flood of iniquity, few were labouring arduously and effectively; but around them was this vast and troubled ocean of depravity; foaming and dashing still. A voice seemed to sound in my ears, "Why go ... anywhere else, to find souls that need the gospel? Here they are, tens and thousands at your very door. Preach to them, the

unsearchable riches of Christ. I will help you—your needs shall be supplied."[33]

Further representing the complete hopelessness of this context, *The Christian Mission* magazine in 1869 published the following advertisement. A clear call to action is evident, driven by a vision that the life-giving hope of the gospel might attack the societal and moral injustices of the day:

OLD MEN

Are being dragged down in anguish to the grave by godless children.

WOMEN

Utterly disgraced, debased, ruined, bruised, with disheveled locks and torn clothing are rolling about the streets of every large town.

LITTLE CHILDREN

Are not merely being starved, crushed and beaten to death, but many of them are being polluted with bad language and every sort of infamy. Against all this, the energetic protests of God and his saints for ages has been unheeded.

SONS OF GOD

Arise to drive back the hellish armies which perpetuate daily these horrors. For God and home and country arise! Arise! and let your deadliest assaults be continually directed against the Prince of the power of the air.[34]

While most people would have suggested the challenge was too great and the social problems absolutely insurmountable, William Booth boldly declared to his wife, "Kate, I have found my destiny. These are the people for whose salvation I have been longing all these years."[35] George Scott Railton, William's right-hand commissioner, recorded Catherine's initial response:

> I remember the emotion that this produced in my soul.
> I sat gazing into the fire and the Devil whispered to me,
> "This means another departure, another start in life!" The
> question of our support constituted a serious difficulty....
> Nevertheless, I did not answer discouragingly. After a
> momentary pause for thought and prayer, I replied, "Well if
> you feel you ought to stay, stay. We have trusted the Lord
> *once* for our support and we can trust him *again*.[36]

Catherine moved on from this moment in time to be an aggressive advocate for the poor, with pronounced sensitivity toward the unjust treatment of women and children. Roger Green references Catherine's first visit to a meeting of the Midnight Movement for the Fallen Women at which two to three hundred prostitutes were present. She spoke to them so fervently, as one sinful woman to another, that some were inspired to change their ways. This was Catherine's introduction to the cruelty directed toward women in England.[37] As her consciousness awakened toward these realities, it was evident that the Army mother embraced her husband's calling as her own. This became a point of stimulus for her preaching. As this evolved, it cannot be overlooked how much Catherine contributed to the socio-political climate of her day, arguing for the equal rights of women; thus earning the freedom for all Salvationist women to take their place in the pulpit.[38]

In view of this historical narrative, we are led to question what this early form of preaching would have looked like without the burden of the cultural context weighing so heavily upon the hearts of William and Catherine Booth. While we can only speculate from our current cultural address, we cannot help but wonder whether the energy and passion that drove this expression of preaching would have been so pronounced if the context had been different. Human need is a tremendously powerful motivator. The plight of those trapped within the darkness of their societal demise gave the Booths clarity of message toward their intended audience. Both sensitivity and sympathetic understanding toward the state of the marginalized shaped William and Catherine's approach. The content of their sermons was fashioned by a clear vision of the needs of the people. There was a mandate to show the relevance of the gospel to effect change and transformation of life, even in the most desperate of situations. The Booths' homiletic had this perspective in clear view. The depth of degradation and suffering that existed in the East End of London forms a frame around this portrait of early Salvation Army preaching. Context is what holds the picture together and provides both clarity and rationale for the preaching of a disturbing gospel. The desperate cries of suffering humanity would forever ring in the ears of the Booths, motivating them with earnest and passionate energy to get gospel truth into the hearts of the people.

Today's preachers are challenged to recognize that an emphasis toward *contextual preaching* is not a new concept. While contemporary voices such as Leonora Tubbs call preachers to not only exegete a biblical text, but also to examine the contextual context from which listeners are coming,[39] William and Catherine Booth could clearly say, "We've been there and we've already done that!" Cultural and contextual analysis in preaching was not a new phenomenon for the Booths. They deeply understood how important these concepts were in defining the shape and design of ministry for the Army in its earliest days.

The Influence of American Revivalism

As previously identified, when William and Catherine Booth became aware of God's call upon their lives to preach the gospel of Jesus Christ, and it was confirmed to whom they must preach, they did not have the benefit of applying to a local seminary for ministry training. Their context did not afford an opportunity for formal courses in hermeneutics, theology, biblical interpretation or even homiletical theory. Yet the Booths were not without significant influences that would speak to their development as preachers.

The influence of American Evangelist James Caughey (1810-1891) becomes a key link in this unfolding story. In 1846, Caughey visited Nottingham, England, conducting revival meetings. It was at this time that William Booth experienced the fiery preaching of this revivalist's oratory. Influenced by Caughey's uncompromising realism, William went to as many services as possible. Joining his voice in the great battle hymns of Charles Wesley, he witnessed scenes of conversion that were passionately moving, including the conversion of many of his neighbours and personal friends who were experiencing new birth. "Here at last was religion in action, the real living religion of his dreams," and to this end William could scarcely think of anything else.[40]

Recognizing the tremendous impact James Caughey's ministry had upon William, and subsequently upon Catherine,[41] we see a form of modeling that Caughey provided for the Booth's preaching. Evidence of this is best found in Caughey's own work, *Methodism in Earnest*, in which the history of the British Revival of the 1840s is recorded. It is significant to note the manner in which Caughey's method and philosophy became mirrored by the Booths in their own practice and writings. The connection was evident within Caughey's assertive claim that the purpose of preaching was to *awaken sinners and bring penitents to God*. Representing the strength of his convictions, bluntly Caughey would question fellow preachers: "What are you aiming at in preaching; for what purpose do you yet enter the pulpit? Is it not to bring sinners to repentance?"[42] This was a theme both William and Catherine would later embrace in their own preaching, but the emphasis was first modelled to them by James Caughey.

In referencing an evangelistic campaign Caughey conducted in the north of England, commentators spoke of "sinners being battered by the artillery of the law and assailed on every side by the offers of the gospel." While appealing to people's fears, Caughey also gave attention to their hopes. "Hell and its horrors ... and its penalties, glared around; while Calvary and its scenes were held forth as pledges of hope and salvation."[43]

Echoing this "battering of the sinner" theme in order to "awaken consciousness toward salvation," Catherine Booth said:

Oh! People say, you must be very careful, very judicious.
You must not thrust religion down people's throats. Then,
I say, you will never get it down. What! Am I to wait till an
unconverted, Godless man wants to be saved before I try

and save him.... Verily we must *make* them look—tear the bandages off, open their eyes ... let them have no peace until they submit to God and get their souls saved.[44]

Within William and Catherine's subsequent approach to preaching, a marked intensity evolved. People needed to think intentionally about their sinful condition. They needed to look toward Christ and not avoid the difficult themes of hell and eternal damnation. Linking this with the power of the gospel message, William reinforced this emphasis encouraging fellow Salvationists to "strike for the salvation of the sinner whenever you have a chance. Strike out. Strike often. Strike with all your might and be sure you strike in faith."[45] It was subsequently through the example and encouragement of James Caughey that William and Catherine Booth became convinced that they could launch a strategic attack against sin in their own context. In so doing, potentially they would win the masses for Christ.

> The preacher needed to work the battle of the human conscience leaving the listener with no choice but to respond to the gospel truth

The novelty of this approach to preaching, however, cannot be credited fully to the originality of James Caughey. Rather it is another American Revivalist, Charles G. Finney (1792-1875), often called the Father of Modern Evangelism, who must be acknowledged as one of the primary architects of this evangelistically driven homiletic.[46] The Booths thoroughly immersed themselves in Finney's writings and followed his ministry closely. Impressed upon them was the importance of utilizing techniques that would urge sinners toward decision. The preacher needed to work the battle of the human conscience leaving the listener with no choice but to respond to the gospel truth. Finney fervently held to the importance of "never resting satisfied until every excuse of the sinner has been annihilated.... Make the sinner see that all pleas in excuse for not submitting to God are an act of rebellion against him. Tear away the last lie which he grasps in his hand and make him feel that he is absolutely condemned before God.[47]

To extend his thinking further in this area, Finney was the first to utilize the concept of an "anxious seat," a special pew or seat set aside from others where individuals could come and publicly declare their verdict for Christ.[48] This practice was adopted also by William and Catherine Booth, although they substituted the term "penitent form" as a designated place for public commitment.

Another American Revivalist influence upon the Booths came from Phoebe Palmer (1807-1874), "the mother of the American Holiness Movement." Esteemed as both an effective evangelist and prolific writer, Palmer gave much emphasis to the Wesleyan doctrine of Christian perfection. As noted by Murdoch, William and Catherine found within Palmer "... an example of female ministry and an exponent of holiness which fit perfectly with the influence of Caughey and Finney."[49] In 1859, *The Wesleyan Times* reported: "Mrs. Palmer now modestly walks within the rail of the communion, not to preach according to the modern acceptation of the term, but simply to talk to the people, which she does with all the gracefulness of an intelligent and well-educated Christian lady."[50] Catherine read Palmer's writings extensively and followed her progress with great interest.

The ministry of Phoebe Palmer did not always receive favourable reviews, however, and in particular this was emphasized within correspondence coming out of the Newcastle Revival of 1859. Herein, the Reverent Arthur Augustus Rees challenged Mrs. Palmer's right to preach.[51] Catherine was deeply angered if not infuriated by this attack. This stimulated her most notable public defence of female ministry. Women had every right to stand in the pulpit and proclaim the deep truths of the gospel. God did not differentiate by gender when he handed out spiritual gifts; neither was there a classification to be made between male and female persuasion as it related to those who would have the privilege to preach. Catherine's convictions were clearly stated. History would subsequently give testimony to the tremendous influence Catherine Booth had in advocating for the role of the female preacher. In Catherine's opinion, this was to be founded upon more than just passivity and receptivity (meaning women were passive receivers of a gift to preach by influence of the Holy Spirit), as argued by Mrs. Palmer. Rather, Catherine based her platform upon strong biblical principles that gave women every right and authority to preach.[52] The influence of Phoebe Palmer had profound influence upon Catherine, stirring these convictions within her.

With the landscape surrounding the evolving pulpit of William and Catherine Booth, it is evident that the legacy of American Revivalism finds its place in the picture. The Booths "... were products of revival ideas carried to England through the ministry of American preachers, and The Salvation Army became the fruit of that influence."[53] Although there is no evidence to suggest that the Booths ever worked directly with their mentors, influence came through their exposure to their meetings, their books and tracts and their fame.[54] The homiletic of William and Catherine Booth is therefore not a new homiletic, for history clearly reveals the imprints of those who had significant influence in shaping the Salvationist approach to preaching.

Wesleyan Theological Foundations

There is a danger in a study such as this that we might conclude the Booths had a singular focus in understanding their homiletical task; the emphasis being only about preaching salvation to the lost. It is important to recognize, however, that The Salvation Army, since its point of inception, has not only been concerned about *saving the sinner* but also with the necessity of *nurturing the saints toward holiness and Christian perfection.* Both William and Catherine believed that it was not enough just to get a person saved—but more importantly how to keep them saved. How could new converts grow in Christian faith, not only maintaining but also strengthening the experience of full salvation? Cyril Barnes in *The Founder Speaks Again,* highlights William's earnest emphasis of this theme:

> We are a salvation people—this is our specialty—getting saved and keeping saved, and then getting somebody else saved and then getting saved ourselves more and more,

until full salvation on earth makes the heaven within, which is finally perfected by the full salvation without, on the other side of the river."[55]

Evidently, for William, the experience of *full salvation* was linked directly with an understanding of what it meant for believers to grow in the grace and knowledge of the Lord Jesus Christ. As a result of this focus, Salvationists gathered regularly for holiness meetings, usually on a Sunday morning. Specific objectives impacted the substance and design of preaching in these services. In *Orders and Regulations for Officers*, 1921, we find these goals for the holiness meeting:

To lead God's people into the enjoyment of holiness. To instruct those who possessed this blessing, how to enjoy it, showing them how to discern and resist evil, understand God's will and fight for souls.[56]

In this perspective, it is easy to trace the influence and theological persuasion of John Wesley (1703-1791). William and Catherine had studied Wesley's works thoroughly. They wholeheartedly endorsed his proposed two-step process of salvation: first, conversion as a remedy for basic human sinfulness and, second, a perfecting and empowering experience that brought more godliness to human behaviour.[57] This second experience was subsequently termed "entire sanctification, holiness, Christian perfection, or (in John Wesley's simple phrase) 'perfect love.' "[58]

Both William and Catherine were adamant in pointing to the centrality of this doctrinal emphasis for preaching purposes. The strength of William's conviction is obvious in his address at the Conference of the Christian Mission in January 1877:

Holiness to the Lord is to us a fundamental truth: it stands to the forefront of our doctrines. We write it on our banners. It is in no shape or form an open debatable question as to whether God can sanctify wholly, whether Jesus does save his people *from* their sins. In the estimation of The Christian Mission, that is settled forever, and any evangelist who did not hold and proclaim the ability of

Jesus Christ to save his people to the uttermost from sin and sinning I should consider out of place among us.[59]

Catherine reinforces this theme in an address she gave at Exeter Hall in 1881:

I think it must be self evident to everyone present that it is *the most important question* that can possibly occupy the mind of man—how much like God we can be—how near to God we can come on earth preparatory to our being perfectly like him, and living, as it were, in his very heart for ever and ever in heaven.... That it seems to me should be the attitude of every person who has the Spirit of God—that he should hunger and thirst after it, and feel that he shall never be satisfied till he wakes up in the lovely likeness of the Saviour.[60]

In further probing the theological emphasis of the Booths in this area, the impact of the biblical imperative becomes obvious. As William saw it, holiness was not a side issue or an optional theme. Rather it was a plain emphatic scriptural message, written in God's Book, revealed in God's Person and required of God's people.[61] William recognized the significance of the *spiritual work that could be done by those who possessed this spiritual power* if this experience was embraced fully. In *The East London Evangelist*, 1869, William expressed how those who were actively searching after the experience of holiness became those best able to accomplish mission objectives:

But how much more might be done had you *all* received this Pentecostal baptism *in all its fullness.* If every soul was inflamed, and every lip touched, and every mind illuminated, and every heart purified with the hallowed flame. O what zeal, what self denial, what meekness, what boldness, what holiness, what love would there not be. The whole city would feel it. God's people in every direction would catch the fire and sinners would fall on every side ... all flesh would see the salvation of God.[62]

Later, to his growing number of followers, Booth would say "the full equipment and qualification and guarantee of success in the great work of pulling down the kingdom of Satan, and establishing the kingdom of God is: Brethren be ye holy, and be holy now."[63] In this respect, perhaps a parallel can be found between William Booth and the writer to the Hebrews, for two pronounced perspectives now seem to sit in conversation with each other. *What becomes possible—without holiness? Not eternal relationship with God,* says the writer to the Hebrews, for "without holiness, no one will see the Lord" (Hebrews 12:14b). For William Booth, not even mission in The Salvation Army, *for holiness was that state of Christian experience that qualified Salvationists to engage in mission* and ultimately authenticated the truth of the gospel message proclaimed. Reflecting the character and qualities of God, fuelled by the energy and power of the Holy Spirit, the Salvationist preacher was an impressive presence with which to be reckoned. The substance and sum of the early Booth homiletic embraces the importance of pressing new believers to a deeper experience of the spiritual life. Preaching aimed not only for converts at the penitent form. The goal was to strengthen people for living out this new found faith in the world and making sure they knew how to keep this faith when difficult days came.

To be relevant and effective within today's pulpit, every preacher must have intimate knowledge of his or her audience's story

Conclusion

The preaching of William and Catherine Booth did not evolve from an empty space in time. Rather, when the Booths entered the Victorian pulpit, a multiplicity of influences and experiences accompanied them, and this served to shape the message that emerged. William and Catherine Booth's preaching was firstly defined by a depth of personal experience that sought to witness to the life-changing power of the gospel. Without this foundational element, nothing else would follow in the story.

This was linked with a strong belief system that owned the centrality of Scripture as the divine inspiration of God and the only rule for Christian faith and practice. Subsequently, the voice of context and the cultural address at which the Booths were living, provided direction as to where preaching would go. This was a message that was clearly influenced by its ultimate destination; the suffering poor. We cannot overstate how significant this became. To be relevant and effective within today's pulpit, every preacher must have intimate knowledge of his or her audience's story. This then dictates the shape and design of the sermon. Suffering humanity placed an indelible mark upon the lives of William and Catherine Booth. This was a mark which they would bear faithfully and fervently for the sake of Christ every time they entered the pulpit. It was for the sake of the people and their sins that they faithfully proclaimed the gospel.

Finally, there were those who provided role modelling and tutelage without ever formally enrolling William and Catherine Booth as their students. Here the works of John Wesley, James Caughey, Charles Finney and Phoebe Palmer had significant bearing. Absorbing all they could from these pulpit icons of their day, there was a sense in which William's and Catherine's approach to preaching was not new. Rather, the Booths become an extension of the influence that was sweeping over Victorian England as winds of revival were bringing fresh life and vitality to the Church. William and Catherine caught the energy and fervor of American Revivalism, and this distinguished the kinds of preachers they became. Linking this ultimately with the work of the Holy Spirit, an early Salvation Army homiletic emerges and demands a hearing.

CHAPTER 2

KEEPING EARLY PULPIT FIRES BURNING

GLORY STORIES CAN BE FOUND WITHIN THE HISTORY OF any religious movement. This should not be surprising to us as it is characteristic of basic human nature to represent our successes and accomplishments. Perhaps it serves to validate what we are about, or at the very least, challenges us to remember rich places where God has blessed the work of The Salvation Army. In the case of the early days of our Movement, positive testimonials became a natural outpouring of victories won. Pulpit fires were burning with marked intensity! Elijah Cadman, a converted chimney sweep who became a voice of significant influence during the Army's formative years, gave a stirring witness to the Spirit's work as he observed it:.

> The meeting began, the Holy Spirit came to be our help at the beginning, and at three o'clock the *waves of glory broke over us* [emphasis mine]. When I gave the invitation to those who were seeking to be holy on earth, 700 men and women came down, the men on one side, the women on the other, and the Holy Ghost broke upon them, and fell upon us all in such a manner, it seemed to nearly carry me out of my clothes.... Some jumped, and jumped, till they jumped into the third heaven. When they got the blessing, they swam about the floor in glory. One was a Quaker, who had never quaked till that night.... 'Pull soldiers, pull, pull the glory down' was sung by Major Dowdle, and set

the whole platform in motion, some pulling vigorously at imaginary ropes.[1]

These types of stories can serve to inspire and energize us. We too might find ourselves longing to catch "waves of glory" breaking in upon our own shores of spiritual experience—although, we might be guarded as to how this might be fully expressed in our worship. Rocking platforms, people being almost "carried out of their clothes" and "swimming about the floor in glory" may seem extreme. It may be more than our conservative congregations are prepared to handle! The point, however, is that a certain energy and vitality is represented within these testimonials. There is a deep connection to the Spirit's activity. In places today where spiritual fervour may be waning, what if we could know something of the same power to which early Salvationists gave witness? How might this change some of the places where we serve?

> In places today where spiritual fervour may be waning, what if we could know something of the same power to which early Salvationists gave witness?

While we may elevate these stories as being significant markers of our denominational story, it is important to pursue a balanced perspective in what comes toward us as we turn the pages of our history. There is a need to put the glory stories alongside those accounts that speak to a critical assessment of the early Army's methods. Gordon Moyles provides a helpful treatment of this in his work, *The Salvation Army and the Public*:

Indeed, for the first decade of its existence, the Booth enterprise was considered by most people merely a passing fad—one of the many such religious eccentricities of English life. England was, as the adage went, the "mother-country of religiosities." They came, and they disappeared, as did a new toilet-fashion from Paris or a new opera song from Venice or Milan. The Christian

Mission was therefore largely dismissed as just another sectarian flash-in-the-pan, unworthy of much concern or interest.[2]

Recognizing the skepticism of those outside Salvation Army circles, the critical question became one of survival. What kept this early Salvation Army alive, and more specifically for the purpose of this discussion, what contributed to the sustaining life of its pulpit? What kept pulpit fires burning? To answer this question, we give specific consideration to the guiding principles that fuelled the Booths' approach to preaching. Something kept this homiletic hot! Catherine's approach to preaching survived for 25 years and in William's case, 47 years. While it could be argued that there was an evolution at work within the Booths' preaching (and one would expect this to be true of any preacher), uncompromising values and convictions created a theology of preaching that kept the temperature well elevated in the pulpit. This would seem not only to be characteristic of the Booth years, but ultimately, as will be evidenced later on, these themes threaded their way forward into subsequent chapters of The Salvation Army's story.

Preaching Fuelled by a Philosophy of Aggression

We simply cannot miss it! Undergirding all that comes from the pulpit of William and Catherine Booth is a deep, unrelenting conviction to preach the gospel of Jesus Christ with earnestness and passion! In a 1904 International Staff Conference, William Booth gave the following charge to officers present:

> I cannot help but feel that *God is set on having his message heard* [emphasis mine]. And if you do not gain it for the hearing He desires, some other agency will be raised up by the necessities of the times and the Spirit of

God will spring to the front, take your place there and rob you of your crown.[3]

The Founder went on to address the complacent spirit he observed at that time among those under his command:

There seems to me to be a great deal of lackadaisical, 'take it easy' way of things…. What I plead for in our talking is a *real* declaration of the truth, a *real* attacking of sin, and a *real* urging to the doing of the will of God all the time.[4]

> To leave a real and lasting impression, meant there had to have been a real engagement with the listener's sense of spiritual struggle

While we might wonder how the Founder would address the state of our own pulpits, clear convictions were evident. It was time to get serious about naming the real issues confronting the sinner. William Booth could speak from his own experience as to the importance of this emphasis, given the impact such preaching had upon his own life:

In my younger days I had the opportunity of listening to many preachers, some of them men of considerable ability and celebrity; but I can count on the fingers of my right hand the number of those who made any real and lasting impression on my heart. And the impressions made by that handful of men was produced, not by their Bible or doctrinal knowledge, nor by their learning, nor by their eloquence, nor by their anecdotal, interesting style; but by the earnestness with which they laboured to overcome the restlessness and worldliness of my young heart.[5]

Clearly, William had known what it was like to go away from preaching unaffected, to which many of us might also add our own testimonials. To leave a *real and lasting impression* meant there had to have been a *real engagement* with the listener's sense of spiritual struggle. The preacher aimed to "tell it like it was" even if this meant pushing to places often deemed uncomfortable or "off limits." In this respect, we note a true absence of any emphasis toward seeker sensitivity. Yet this did not close down the early Salvationist pulpit! In fact, it energized it and pushed it forward. The Booths believed that the preacher needed an aggressive approach in the pulpit to make people think about their sins and force them to consider their eternal destination. Commissioner Theodore Kitching (1866-1930), secretary and confidant to both William and Bramwell Booth, captured this sentiment in *The Officer* magazine in 1916. If a "lacksadasical" spirit was developing among Salvation Army troops, Kitching confronted it in this admonition:

> The desired outcome was to get the good news of God's Word deep down inside the people

Show the people their sins—remind them of their coffins—make them think about the judgment bar—tell them of the cleansing blood—picture to them the bliss of the saved and the agony of the lost. Describe hell as unmistakably as Jesus did. Say "damned" as much as He did—tell them that heaven and hell last forever ... push it into the people till it pricks their hearts, and the best preacher is one that pricks the most hearts.[6]

Ultimately, the goal was to urge the truth of the gospel message upon the audience and press for a decision. The desired outcome was to get the good news of God's Word deep down inside the people. William reinforced this emphasis within directives he gave to field officers for the preparation of public addresses:

My object is to get my audience right with God for time and eternity in order that they may bless others. The field officer must endeavour to convict the sinners present— we must make them feel that they are wicked. We must dig it into them. *I want to dig it into you.* Where are the preachers or revivalists who make people realize that they are wicked? There is very little preaching today. You must make them feel that they are in danger of hell.[7]

While some today might argue such an approach to preaching was too strong, perhaps even to some degree abusive and not respectful of audience comfort levels, for William and Catherine Booth there was no middle ground. Lost souls were to be snatched from the pit of sin and raised up to see the possibility of new life in Christ. With this end in mind, the early homiletic of The Christian Mission and subsequently The Salvation Army found its life and vitality.

Preaching Fuelled by Avoidance of Churchliness

We do not wade very far into this place of history without realizing there was something to which this early Salvation Army homiletic was reacting! Most clearly defined, it was a marked intent to avoid the appearance of churchliness in preaching. This first surfaced in the language used to speak about preaching. There are few references to the word *sermon* within early Salvation Army sources. The phrase *public address* was the more popular way to identify what the Salvationist preacher delivered from the pulpit. In 1913, *The Field Officer* magazine published the following sentiment, which helps to explain this observed phenomenon:

I much dislike the use of the words *sermon* and *preaching* in respect of the addresses of Army officers. They smack too much of ministerialism, of formal sermonizing and are something of an affection on our lips.[8]

We sense the greater debate surrounding this issue as we navigate a distinction between that of being a "church" versus that of being an "Army." Brigadier Bramwell Taylor (an officer who served in varying capacities in the early Army) captured the difference that he argued was to be preserved:

> We are separate from the world and a distinctly separate force in the realm of religion ... we are an Army, not a church ... the idea of sermons being preached from our platform is quite incongruous.... Our term is "songs" not "hymns."[9]

With this understood, the Booths were convinced that when the preacher stood to address the congregation, there was a need to represent a common people's gospel. What was said had to be understood; otherwise, the preacher's efforts were wasted. *Simplicity of approach was to be the guiding rule.* In his personal memoirs, Commissioner J. Evan Smith, once private secretary to William Booth, commented on the Founder's preaching:

> The Founder never bothered with theological discourses. Life was too short; his message too urgent. People were going down into perdition and he must hurry to save them. He had more than 300 addresses in his subject file cabinet, alphabetically indexed and numbered, all of them with a vital message.... He was often dramatic on the platform and this was emphasized at times by the repetition of words or phrases.... No milk-and-water expressions fell from the lips of William Booth! There was no whittling down of the truth! Passionately strong in his denunciation of sin, he was equally so in his appeals to the sinner to give it up.[10]

In this respect, we see a tension developing between that which was considered mainstream preaching and the kind of preaching the Booths were taking into the slums of East End London. The Salvation Army "way of preaching" was to be different from what might have been experienced in any other established pulpit of the day. To preach simply and relevantly to the suffering poor, officer-preachers had to avoid anything that seemed formal, liturgical or academic. Intellectual preaching that aimed only to reach the head failed to recognize that the ultimate destination was really the heart. *The Field Officer* magazine, in September 1909, reflected this emphasis:

> Preaching that wins souls ... is not the moral essay, or the intellectual or semi-intellectual kind of preaching most generally heard throughout the world today, that is to save men; for thousands of such sermons move and convert no one. Nor is it a mere noisy declamation called a sermon— noisy because empty of all earnest thought and true feeling; but it must be the kind which Peter speaks when he writes of "them that preached the gospel ... with the Holy Ghost sent down from heaven."[11]

To preach simply and relevantly to the suffering poor, officer-preachers had to avoid anything that seemed formal, liturgical or academic

In response to this, the question lingers; did this mean that this early form of preaching was devoid of theological substance? Was there a sense of depth within this homiletic? Were converts nurtured into the deep truths of Scripture? In 1882, an early Salvationist preaching primer circulated, entitled *The Question of Questions*. It advocated that "the message had to be concise, simple and not given to abstruse doctrines that if provable by reason, could not be proved but by the intellectual."[12] In this respect, Salvation Army preaching gave itself to this experiential emphasis in the formative years of the Movement. The truth of the gospel needed to be *taught* in a manner that could be *caught*, for only as listeners were able to see the relevance of God's Word to their lives would preaching be successful. This became a recurring emphasis within a 1918 issue of *The Officer* magazine, which offered some preaching helps for the Book of Revelation:

To *hear,* to *read,* and to *keep* the words of this book require some study and perhaps we may best obtain this promised blessing, and avoid all the controversies over which generations of Bible students have spent their time, if as simple, unlearned people, we keep mainly to the parts of our Lord's revelation which we *can* grasp. This applies especially to the messages given to 'The Seven Churches of Asia.' These seem marvelously applicable to Salvation Army Corps today.[13]

A new tension emerges for us in the assessment of this emphasis. Did this early homiletic (or preaching approach) risk insufficient acknowledgment of the intellectual capacity of its audience? Was there a sense in which the gospel was unnecessarily simplified? Were early congregants, in fact, capable of embracing a more complex presentation? The limited educational background of many of the Army's first converts became an influencing factor in the decision of early Salvationist preachers to avoid pulpit formality. This meant Salvationist preaching would ultimately seek to represent *liveliness in proclamation* that would in turn point people to the *life-giving power of the gospel.* An advertisement for a 1915 Sunday afternoon service provides a further window into this truth:

Bring Baby and the others to our Family Gatherings in The Salvation Army Citadel, High Street, every Sunday afternoon from 3 to 4. Bright Music and Singing, Short Spicy Speaking, A Hearty Welcome, Not a Dull Minute out of Sixty.[14]

No doubt this was not the kind of sign hanging on the doorposts of churches down the road from the Army corps! Early Salvation Army preaching was defined and energized by its avoidance of churchliness. It grew with conviction and resolve, recognizing the importance of a simplistic approach to reach those who would otherwise be overwhelmed with weighty theological discourse.

Preaching Fuelled by Missional Focus

If aggression and avoidance of churchliness are the first two logs set in place by the Booths to keep pulpit fires burning, then the energy that comes from an intentional focus toward mission followed closely behind. History presents a very clear picture of how The Salvation Army in its formative years adopted a philosophy that said: "By any means, let Christ be preached." Undergirding this philosophy was a belief system that recognized the need to capture the attention of sleeping sinners and stab them awake with conviction of their sin. Although not ever directly named in this way, it was as if early Salvationists set out on a mission to sound an eschatological alarm clock in the ears of their listeners. The end was coming! Eternal judgment was just over the next horizon. *Orders and Regulations* given to field officers in 1922 reinforced this theme:

"By any means, let Christ be preached"

> The field officer will find the great bulk of unconverted people totally unconcerned about religion. They are as men who slumber; their eyes are closed to the destruction ahead of them, and like men who sleep, they dream; dream of long life, pleasure, wealth, ease, ambition and other things—of everything save the dark storm of wrath and ruin that lies just ahead of them. If ever their thoughts turn to the necessity of Salvation, they console themselves with the illusion that they will have many more opportunities, or with some other equally foolish excuse.... The duty of the field officer is to startle them and make them look away from this world to the next.[15]

Recognizing the significance of this mandate, William and Catherine Booth inspired within their followers the capacity to think outside of conventional norms for the purpose of soul saving. Describing William's style, approach and modelling, British reporter Sir Philip Gibbs (1877-1962), offered the following as a eulogy to the life of the Founder:

He used every art and trick of oratory, every crude and vulgar method to "win souls to God." He would jibe and jest at them with a biting humour. He would use the slang of the slum, and the cant of the thieves' alley. He would sing to them and dance to them, in a kind of religious ribaldry. He would make himself a buffoon for the love of God, and by these methods he would drag people up from the depth of misery, drag them by the scruff of the neck from the mire to cleanliness, give them back their manhood and womanhood, and fan into a flaming torch the little spark of divinity which never goes out in the human heart.[16]

Perhaps one of the best places the early Salvation Army displayed its innovative thinking was in its open-air work. Story upon story reveals the manner in which early Salvationists sought to capture the attention of people in the cathedral of the great outdoors. The Army's militant structure, complete with uniforms, flags and marching brass bands could create quite a stirring procession, which would end ultimately in a setting where the gospel could be preached. Subsequently, the bass drum would be turned over on its side to make a penitent form[17] and many early converts found salvation kneeling at this make-shift altar in the great outdoors. Christian Mission reports highlighted how early Salvationists encountered their most intense persecution in these settings, as evidenced in the following 1874 monthly summary:

In the history of the past month, one of the chief features has been the violent opposition our brethren have had to encounter while conducting their meetings in the open air, the police, the publicans and lewd followers of the baser sort, having in turns, and, in some instances, all seemed to combine to defeat and drive us from the ground....
At Poplar a good deal of trouble has been experienced. The roughs, on one occasion, formed themselves into a band, and charging down the street with most discordant, deafening cries and threatenings, endeavoured to break up the meeting. Our brethren, however ... stood firm; other friends came up to assist, and after some time silence

was obtained. The enemies listened, and at the close the ringleader, stretching his hand over the heads of the crowd, expressed his regret and asked for forgiveness.[18]

While most would be tempted in this kind of context to give up the battle for fear of personal safety, there is something in this story that remains energized and focused. Persecution drove early Salvationists toward complete dependence upon God and reinforced for them the special mission that was theirs to publish Jesus Christ in the open air:

"God did not want another church when he created The Salvation Army amid the soot and slime of London's East End. The skyline was already crowded with steeples...."

And shall we not give ourselves afresh to this work.... This is our special vocation ... so much the need for us to redouble our diligence while so many thousands are ignorant of their condition, and know not of salvation from sin and hell through the precious blood, *and while they will stand to hear this glad news,* neither publicans nor infidels, nor any kind of wind or weather, must cause us to cease crying in the open air, "Behold the Lamb of God, that taketh away the sin of the world!"[9]

Preaching Fuelled by a Unique Ecumenical Calling

In 1929, a Centenary Celebration commemorated the 100th anniversary of William Booth's birth (1829-1912).[20] At this gathering, the British prime minister and the president of the National Council of the Free Church Federation offered notable tributes. From these speeches, there was a clear representation of the *unique ecumenical calling* owned by the Founder from the Army's earliest point of inception. This uniqueness of calling became yet another log added to the fire which served to advance the Booths' early homiletic further into history. Herein, we identify how a strong sense of ecumenical distinctiveness defined the kind of preaching that was coming from Salvationist pulpits. The Salvation Army was not meant to be like any other church of its time. General Albert Orsborn articulated this emphasis when he said, "God did not want another church when he created The Salvation Army amid the soot and slime of London's East End. The skyline was already crowded with steeples...."[21] British Prime Minister Stanley Baldwin was quick to point out the way in which William Booth represented this distinction in his life's work:

> To have churches was not necessarily the same thing as to have religion, and that you might have in human life respectability and sobriety but that they really might be the cloak of a sham inside. This was the reason why he [William Booth] went out from the church to preach, and chose for his hurch the theatre, the prison, the highway, and the market-place.[22]

The Booths recognized a void that the mainline churches were not filling. They identified an emptiness of experience that was caught up in a ritualistic routine rather than a real experience of *red-hot religion*. This pressed the Booths' calling toward something different and it was this sense of spiritual vocation that had impact upon their preaching. There were specific needs that were unaddressed by other religious institutions. God was setting The Salvation Army apart to engage in a unique mission that would demonstrate special sensitivity toward the poor and the disenfranchised. The Salvationist preacher had a distinct contribution to make toward the building of the kingdom of God. Too many people were sitting on the margins of religion, and it seemed few influences were changing this landscape. In this respect, this early homiletic sustained its momentum and vibrancy because those who owned it recognized the potential for its unique influence.

Offering further critique on the ecumenical landscape of the Booths' day, The Rev. Principal Thomas Philips, president of the

National Free Church Council, suggested that only when William Booth stepped outside the established churches of his day did God begin to use him. Ultimately, it was a clear sense of ecumenical distinction that propelled William and Catherine Booth forward:

> Hence we are faced with this tremendous fact: That at a time when organized Christianity was thought to be essential, perhaps the greatest work was done *outside* the Christian Church, by a Christian man whom the Christian Church excommunicated.... We are timid ... we like to keep the Devil at a respectable distance. We believe in fortifications—great churches, great services and great preachers. We are inclined as churches to dig ourselves into trenches. William Booth was "over the top" [of the trench] every time.[23]

With battle gear and armour firmly secured, William Booth's Army did not fear the enemy but rather boldly stood to oppose the forces of sin plaguing suffering humanity. With this approach to preaching, they marched forward, focused upon a conviction that clearly said, "We have a message that cannot be silenced."

Preaching Fuelled by a Deep Burden for People

Often there come points in our experience as preachers where we tire of people and the demands ministry makes upon us. These moments often bring about negativity toward those for whom we have pastoral charge. While dark days of discouragement shadowed both William and Catherine, this had little impact upon their resolve to keep ministering to human brokenness. As we enter fully into the Booths' life story, it is apparent how deeply they cared about people and how great a burden they carried for the salvation and spiritual well-being of others. The strength of this focus and conviction remained with them until the dying moments of their lives. Catherine's farewell message, presented at the twenty-fifth anniversary celebration of The Salvation Army, at the Crystal Palace, conveyed her deep affection for her people:

My Dear Children and Friends:
My place is empty, but my heart is with you. You are my
joy and my crown. Your battles, sufferings and victories
have been the chief interest of my life these past 25 years.
They are so still. Go forward! Live holy lives. Be true to the
Army. God is your strength. Love and seek the lost; bring
them to the blood. Make the people good; inspire them
with the Spirit of Jesus Christ. Love one another; help your
comrades in dark hours. I am dying under the Army flag;
it is yours to live and fight under.... I send you my love and
blessing—Catherine Booth.[24]

Recounting the final moments of her father's life, Lucy Booth
Hellberg (youngest daughter to the Booths), spoke at the Founder's
memorial service. What followed was a vivid representation of just
how heavy the burden was that William Booth carried for suffering
humanity:

He had no worry or anxiety or fear for himself—all his
thought and anxiety was for people for whom he had lived.
In another of his half-conscious moments near the end I
heard him whisper, "Oh to save these people!" and again,
"What good of a meeting if it is not hot? Do you hear what
I say?" "Yes, General," I replied. "Not a bit good if it isn't
hot," he repeated. Once I heard him cry out, "Oh I can't
bear it. I cannot carry any longer on my poor heart the
sins and sorrows of the people." I felt in my heart he had
carried them long enough. I leaned over and said, "General,
dear, you need not carry them any longer. Lay them down
and sleep."[25]

Such testimonies bear witness to that which lay buried deep
within two extraordinary soul winners who gave themselves fully to
the work of God. The need for human recognition or homiletical distinction did not enter into their ministry's frame of reference. All
they gave came because of what lay rooted deeply within them. This

not only shaped the content of their preaching but it gave their message energy and life. The homiletic of William and Catherine Booth survives its time and space because of a burning passion carried for all peoples to get right with God. If the Booths could have seen this great mission achieved in their lifetime, how great the celebration would have been. Yet as they departed from this world, there was a sense in which they had to recognize something good had begun in them and extended through them. We are challenged to respond to what has been set before us; for that which might be perceived as a smoldering sacred flame, sparks the possibility of new fire into our pulpits. And so we ask, what shall we do with this disturbing gospel especially after we have witnessed the effect it has had upon the formation of our Movement?

Conclusion

The preceding pages have sought to paint a picture. The challenge now is to draw together all of the brush strokes on the canvas and identify the final portrait. The early homiletic of The Salvation Army, as represented in the preaching ministry of William and Catherine Booth, was kept alive and nurtured by specific convictions and methodologies. Firstly, *a philosophy of aggression defined early Salvation Army preaching.* Without compromise, the full gospel of Jesus Christ had to be proclaimed, even that which the listener would rather NOT hear! A forthright declaration of truth was to be made, its forceful attack on sin awakening listeners to their desperate need of salvation. Confrontation was required to make people think about their options as it related to their eternal destination. What might eternity look like if their lives were not right with God?

Secondly, *preaching was fuelled by an avoidance of churchliness,* which required the preacher to engage simplicity of approach. The Booths understood the need to avoid heady theological discourse, if common, unlearned, people were to embrace the truth proclaimed. In achieving this, listeners would know first-hand what it meant to become a new creation in Christ and subsequently, they would discover personal and profound ways to live out the gospel in their world.

Thirdly, the Booths saw their *preaching ministry defined by a unique ecumenical calling.* Stepping into the gaps of their cultural context, where no other Movement of that day dared to go, they aimed their preaching at those who were on the margins of religion. This brought a deep sense of purpose to all that took place in the pulpit. Those beyond respectable religious circles desperately needed the Salvationist voice to bring hope and good news into the darkness of their circumstances. To this great cause, the Booths gladly signed their names and invited others to follow.

Finally, and perhaps most significantly, *the sensitivity and longing of both William and Catherine Booth for the salvation of the lost,* reminds us that *preaching was and always will be a pastoral task.* The agonizing and longing of the Booths for those outside an experience of faith remained, until the very end of their days, a driving and motivating force for preaching. Thus the Booths would offer one more sermon and one more invitation to the cross of Jesus Christ, if it meant a lost soul would find his or her way to the Saviour. Recognizing within every human being a "tiny spark of divinity" that could lead to godly living, William and Catherine Booth pushed the early Army forward on its knees, praying, preaching and believing salvation was possible; even for those to whom society had already issued final judgment.

With these insights in view, the question remains whether this particular brand of preaching has any value beyond its own historical context. Are the principles defining this early form of Salvation Army preaching transferable to a contemporary setting? One cannot ignore the fact that ultimately this form of preaching does present a very confrontational approach. The hard claims of the gospel are not to be ignored, but are to be presented with the intent of "annihilating the sin within a sinner's life!"[26] What does the voice of this homiletic offer the Church of today as we grapple with the challenge of preaching these same disturbing and sometimes offensive truths of the gospel?

In a society seeking world peace, how does the contemporary preacher grapple with the violence of Scripture, that proclaims a suffering Messiah who dies at the hands of religious leaders? How does today's preacher call a self-centred society to a life of sacrifice and the ultimate forgiveness of our enemies, no matter how great the offense? How does this gospel connect with realities of suicide bombers flying airplanes into buildings, causing irreparable loss and grief? In a consumer-driven age that believes he who wins is the one with the most toys, how does one reasonably argue that it is easier for a camel to go through the eye of a needle than for a rich man to enter into the kingdom of heaven? How do we proclaim this message, which clearly argues all have fallen out of God's favour (see Romans 3:23) and are in need of saving grace? How can the homiletic (or the preaching approach) of William and Catherine Booth now extend its brush strokes into the complex cultural landscape of a postmodern/post-Christian setting? Is there anything in this homiletic that can live on?

CHAPTER 3

VICTORIAN ENGLAND
WARMS UP TO THE GOSPEL

AT THE TURN OF THE 19TH CENTURY, A MAN THAT we will representatively call Michael lives in the throes of monumental change. The major event shaping history is the effect of the Industrial Revolution now taking up full residence in Victorian England. Sensing the economic advancement that new factory work could offer and the hope of a better life, Michael takes his wife and five children; he uproots them from their country home and goes to make his fortune in the city. Once inside this new reality, Michael is confronted with grave financial strain, long work days, unsafe working conditions and minimal time with his family.[1] At the end of the day, when he does make it home, he is forced to squeeze into a tiny one room flat that he occupies with both his own family and his in-laws. The roof leaks when it rains; a chilling wind blows through broken windows; mould grows on the walls; when he goes to buy his groceries, he is forced by factory management to purchase from the most expensive merchants. While he recognizes the injustice of this arrangement, he knows that if he does not purchase from the family firm of his employer, he will himself be without work.[2] The crowding, the noise, the lack of privacy finally convince Michael it is easier not to come home after his shifts. Gradually, he finds solace with his drinking buddies and the ladies of the street. To help pay for both his bills and his own habits, he sells his oldest daughter into prostitution.[3] It is one less mouth to feed and it puts money in his pocket. Without even realizing how it happened, Michael (and others) became another statistic within the social story of Victorian England. Into this context, William and Catherine Booth dared to bring the message of a disturbing gospel.[4]

Historical sources witness to the credibility of this reality, perhaps better captured in Robert Langbaum's work, *The Victorian Age,* in which he offers both a demographic description and social commentary on the parish community to which a local preacher ministered:

> The parish of Bethnal Green contains 1,400 houses, inhabited by 2,795 families, or about 12,000 persons. The space upon which this large population dwells is less than 400 yards (1,200 feet) square, and in this overcrowding it is nothing unusual to find a man, his wife, four or five children, and sometimes both grandparents, all in one single room, where they eat, sleep and work.... I have never seen such complete helplessness of the poor.... Not one father of a family in ten in the whole neighbourhood has other clothing than his working suit, and that is as bad and tattered as possible; many indeed have no other covering for the night than these rags, and no bed save a sack of straw or shavings.[5]

Today, more than 200 years later, The Salvation Army continues to encounter similar stories; Michael still has descendants living at similar addresses, culturally speaking. Within our inner cities and beyond, many continue to mirror the reality of Michael's suffering. They are often the discarded of society and we find them caught in the vices of crime, poverty, alcohol, drug abuse or human trafficking. While once dreaming of success and professional advancement, Michael's descendants struggle to know where their next meal will come from and whether they will make the count for a bed each night at the local Salvation Army hostel.

In these scenarios, we find common ground between the Victorian pulpit and the audience the preacher addresses today. Both past and current contexts give ongoing witness to the fact that human trouble never falls off the preacher's radar screen. Current social commentary still speaks to the plight of the homeless, the disadvantaged, the addict, the alcoholic, and those entrapped within systems of human trafficking. Suffering and sin have not left us alone; they still know our address regardless of the years that have lapsed. We find proof of this in our newspapers, on our news broadcasts and in the lines of people that wait for help in our social services centres. It is here that the Booth homiletic is able to initiate conversation with today's preacher, affirming our shared perspective: We still have a sin problem! Many of us might wish for a different assessment. Yet this reality defines the common ground upon which all human beings stand, no matter what login we use to access our historical address. Our commonality with the Victorian era, however, sits in contrast with notable differences.

Religious Authority in Victorian England—Let Church be Church

Although religious expression was richly diverse, it was a very important element of Victorian society. From the high liturgical nature of Church of England worship, to the varied practices of both Protestant traditions and dissenting movements, it was argued that "Christianity in an Oxford common room or a cathedral close bore little resemblance to that in a Primitive Methodist community or a Salvation Army meeting."[6] In short, Victorian religion reflected the diversity of Victorian society. Robert Ensor, in *The Oxford History of England, 1870-1914*, suggests that "no one will ever understand Victorian England who does not understand that it was one of the most religious countries the world has ever known."[7] Why, at this juncture of history, was this true? What was it about organized religious expression that created such a magnetic draw of society? In order to answer this question, it is critical to understand that for the Victorian middle to upper class, religion was a means through which respectability was defined. Christopher Hibbert, in *The Daily Life of*

> "No one will ever understand Victorian England who does not understand that it was one of the most religious countries the world has ever known"

Victorian England, offers the following commentary:

> Christianity was of profound importance to him [middle-class man]. Its precepts permeated his nursery. At his public school he was told that ... "religious and moral principles" were above all required of him: they were even more important than "gentlemanly conduct," which was itself to be more highly regarded than intellectual ability. In his adult life he was conscious always that the probity of his conduct was God's concern: straight dealing would be rewarded, dishonesty punished in the afterlife.[8]

Strict observance of the Sabbath gave clear witness to the elevated place of religion in Victorian society. A Swiss tourist visiting London in 1851 reflects this emphasis within personal musings:

> I ... walked down Cheapside which is quite a long street. I would have liked to have gone into a coffee-house for a glass of ale or claret but all the shops were hermetically sealed.... Even the front door of my own hotel was locked and if one knew the secret one could turn the right knob and effect the entry.... On the return to my hotel I asked for my bill as I had been accustomed to settling my account every day. But the innkeeper politely asked me to *wait until Monday* [emphasis mine].[9]

While the voice of this tourist reflects the high value businesses placed upon a day of Sabbath rest, this emphasis was equally stringent within private homes. Hibbert recounts the Sunday memories of one middle-class Victorian child:

> [Sunday was] a day when Papa was home ... on Sundays we would all be around the fire. We had tea in the dining room. There were four different kinds of jam. After tea he read to us and gave us toffees. I remember how carefully we unwrapped the paper so as not to make a noise. We were not allowed to play ordinary games on Sundays. We would bring our dolls downstairs and have them in the drawing room. We used to take turns sitting on his knee....

He used to tell us stories.[10]

As Victorian family life defined itself by the routine reverencing of Sunday activity, the observance of Sabbath almost became a religion in itself. There was a definite expectation for a specific code of behaviour. Both the young and the old were to adhere to strict patterns of regularity. No games of any kind were to be played; no field sports; no entertainment given, whether public or private. Even books were censored for the day and novels were banned. Only the Bible or other serious, preferably religious, works were allowed. "The habit of setting apart one rest-day in the week for religion and serious thinking was said to have been responsible for deepening the character of the nation."[11] (One might wonder what such a discipline would contribute to the moral and social fibre of today if we were to return to such a disciplined focus!)

> The routine of disciplined religion became not only a desired expression of how Victorian people lived, but it brought a sense of rhythm and definition to daily life

This sense of religious expression further sustained itself by its vigorous amount of external observance. This was especially true in evangelical circles where people spent an extravagant amount of time in organized prayer, praise and preaching events. Within typical English villages, practically all people above infancy attended church or chapel, some even two to three times a day. The children went twice to Sunday schools and throughout the week chapels often held prayer meetings and a regular weeknight service–both being numerously attended.[12] It is from this religious structure that The Salvation Army obviously finds modeling for its own practices of worship.

The routine of disciplined religion became not only a desired expression of how Victorian people lived, but it brought a sense of rhythm and definition to daily life. It brought stability to society. When older, pre-existing agencies of social control, such as local police and judicial courts, struggled to have impact upon the social order, some looked to the internal disciplines inculcated by religion to make a difference. Others found in dissenting religious institutions the means to press both their political and social agendas.[13] This became significantly important as large cities dealt with issues of overpopulation, insufficient health care, lack of adequate sanitation and the overall extreme poverty of the masses. Within this complex and taxing historical narrative, the Church was an integral part of Victorian DNA. A natural outcome of this was a deep sense of respect for the authority of the Church, which subsequently extended to local parish clergy. In this respect, commentary from the Victorian age speaks to the high level of esteem and trust automatically given by society to clergy. These were individuals set apart from the local community, and what a clergyman was mattered just as much as what he did. He was to be a "living pattern to Christians, a living rebuke to sinners ... in short a man of consecrated character" who would speak into the moral fibre of the community through his Christian influence.[14]

The trusted role of local clergy is underlined further by the way in which wayward and delinquent men used this trust to advance their own devious causes. We see this especially in the manner by which keepers of brothels sought to lure young girls into their grip. In a back-handed way, the following affirms the elevated role of preachers and the way in which their words were to be trusted.

> The getting of fresh girls takes time, but it is simple and easy enough ... I have gone and courted girls in the country under all kinds of disguises, occasionally assuming *the dress of a parson* [emphasis mine] and made them believe I intended to marry them, and so got my power to please a good customer. After courting my girl for a time, I propose to bring her to London to see the sights. I bring her up, take her here and there, giving her plenty to eat and drink—especially drink.... I contrive it so that she loses her last train.... I offer her nice lodgings for the night ... my client gets his maid.[15]

The manner in which religious authority was held in such high regard remains noteworthy. The voice of local clergy immediately had hearing, simply because of the status and respect society was willing to offer. How unfortunate and disappointing it must have been when this trust was compromised! While recognizing this tension, one fact remains. When the Victorian preacher spoke the truths of Scripture, it was not necessary to seek permission for a hearing. It was not necessary to debate the overall relevance of the preacher's office, nor did anyone question the infringement of human rights. Victorian society had chosen tolerance of religious perspective and this facilitated an embracing of the values the Church represented. Paul Wilson, in *The Practice of Preaching*, speaks to this reality in referencing the popularity of preaching in recent centuries. Herein it is evident that the preacher was automatically granted considerable authority when there was little distinction between a preacher's opinion and actual fact, when church attendance was a social duty and when, because of lack of formal education, congregations sought information and learning from a communal-shared perspective.[16] These realities created a fertile ground for the Victorian pulpit. Without even having to work at it, the preacher gained an instant hearing, simply by virtue of the office. Cultural norms and societal values affirmed the role of the preacher. The people gave the preacher the authority and right to represent God's voice and to become a source of theological interpretation to them.

Victorian Belief Systems

In seeking to further understand the nature of the socio-religious landscape of Victorian England, due consideration must be given to the effects of *evangelicalism*. Rising historically as a theological movement in the 18th century, evangelicalism made a distinction between the Roman Catholic Church and movements following the tradition of the Protestant Reformation. Asserting strong affinity to the term *gospel*, evangelical preachers believed in the centrality of the doctrine of salvation, defined in the death of Christ, which atoned for human sin. High emphasis was placed upon the need for personal conversion and the centrality of Scripture.[17] It is through the voices of such individuals as John Wesley (1703-1791),

William Wilberforce (1759-1833), William Gladstone (1809-1898), Charles Spurgeon (1843-92) and Charles Finney (1792-1875), to name a few, that the soil was cultivated for evangelicalism to have a significant influence upon Victorian society. Three emphases defined the Victorian belief system. Firstly, there was a literal stress placed upon the Bible. It made the English, the "people of a book." Scripture was the defining rule for action and faith. Secondly, there was certainty attached to the existence of an afterlife of rewards and punishments. This was not a subject for theological debate. If one had asked how 19th-century English merchants earned the reputation of being the most honest in the world, the answer was because hell and heaven seemed as certain to them as tomorrow's sunrise and the Last Judgment as real as the week's balance sheet. Thirdly, it was evident that a guiding assumption directed life and daily activity; the present life was only important as a preparation for eternity.[18] Therefore, it was critical that people consider their eternal destination.

> People understood the existence of the afterlife, with all its possible rewards and punishments, as the way things were

With these emphases noted, it is clearly understandable why the Booths were able to centre their preaching so much in the themes of heaven and hell. Victorian society embraced these beliefs, and life was fashioned in such a way to address the impact of the same. People understood the existence of the afterlife, with all its possible rewards and punishments, as the way things were. This truth had wide acceptance. It became one of the critical reasons why the Booths knew such marked success in their approach to biblical preaching. They did not have to convince their audience of a right perspective; they simply had to get their audience to pay attention to their message.

Breakdown of Social Class

Roger Green, in his work *War on Two Fronts*, says that an outpouring of *individualism* was ushered into Victorian society with the arrival of industrialization. This, too, is an important distinguishing factor of this period in history, as it provides a means toward understanding the subsequent breakdown of social classes and the impact this had upon the preaching task:

> For all the advantages brought about by the Industrial Revolution, it produced a kind of rampant individualism. Individuals were inspired by the thoughts of getting rich, and often this manifested itself in an attitude of self-help and desire to make money. The strong embraced such individualism. The weak were often devastated and abused by it. The weak shared neither the wealth nor the power. As more and more people entered the competitive marketplace, new classes were created. The division between the few rich and the many poor began to break down.[19]

In this context, Victorian England truly became a scenario in which the rich were getting richer and the poor were getting poorer. While the middle to upper classes were readily finding places in religious worship, and saw this as a *respectable* social protocol, this was not the case for the working class poor. Helmstadter and Philips, in *Religion in Victorian Society*, identify how this social reality became an increasingly troubling issue to the established Church and nonconformists alike. The key question addressed was why did the churches not attract the working classes? Why did the poor seem to remain on the fringe, or just beyond, as it related to religious involvement? Toward the middle of the 19th century, both churchmen and dissenters became anxiously aware that large numbers of working class men and women, especially those in large towns, were not associated with any church or chapel. The religious census of 1851 confirmed this worried impression, and during the second half of the century there were many attempts to gain or regain the working class for Christ.[20]

We can only speculate what contributed to this reality. Was this due to the social injustices the rich were imposing on the poor? When the poor attended church services, did they feel welcomed? Did they experience a style of worship that engaged the heart and mind? Or were they challenged to find their way through a dense liturgical fog to which they had limited educational background to navigate? Whatever the contributing factors, we note that within this context of history there was a huge gap between religious expression of the rich and religious expression of those with lesser means. The poor were not finding their way into settings of worship, even though in Victorian society, religion was clearly a defining cultural value that spoke to a certain quality of life. Pamela Walker further qualifies that "if there was a connection of the working class to religion, it was a distant relationship that only looked for the ceremonial rites of passage rather than qualitative membership and involvement. Although most children were baptized and attended Sunday school and the majority of marriages were solemnized in the Church, clergy despaired over the low attendances at church and chapel services."[21] While the services of the Church were utilized for certain rites of passage there was a disconnection of society from the life and fellowship of the local congregation.

William and Catherine Booth responded to this reality with a form of preaching that did not wait for people to enter the doors of an established church. Rather, they took the gospel message into the open air where people were, instead of trying to preach in places where the poor were not.

Influence of Neighbourhood Demographics

The neighbourhood landscape of Victorian England also merits our attention in this discussion. As William and Catherine Booth looked for alternate settings in which to take their message, their landing place became the local neighbourhoods where the poor were living. These communities were distinguished by a rampant presence of poverty, overcrowding and despair. With this in view, we give specific attention to the way in which people spent their time in neighbourhood streets and gathered themselves as a neighbourhood community. Pamela Walker highlights this as she speaks about the manner in which city streets were always well populated, sometimes to the point of overcrowding. People from all classes were found readily in the outdoors journeying to and from work, marketing or visiting with neighbours and friends. London housing was notoriously crowded and whether it was sought after or not, this brought an instant sense of community. One middle-class observer of East London life said: "So many of our people, young and old, passed their time leaning out of windows, sitting on steps, or swarming at play in the middle of the road, that the slightest provocation collected a crowd."[22]

Into this setting, with trumpets blaring and flags waving, the Booths marched with their aggressive message, proclaiming a better life for all, through the saving power of God's grace and truth. An instant hearing was guaranteed, as this particular form of preaching was attentive to how people were organizing themselves within the community context, and how they were naturally congregating in community space.

Conclusion

As the early preaching style of The Salvation Army intersected with the society of Victorian England, four factors contributed to its success. Firstly, the setting into which the Booths heralded the gospel message was favourably disposed towards religion. This led to a high degree of cultural acceptance toward the authority of the Church and the role of clergy. Life fashioned itself routinely to hallow the sacredness of Sunday and the giving of ones' time toward the activities and events of the Church as a cultural norm. In this respect, early preaching in The Salvation Army found fertile ground for ministry and mission. People warmed up to the Booths' gospel.

Secondly, Victorian belief systems embraced the truth the Church proclaimed. There was a clear understanding of the realities of heaven and hell and the punishment and rewards that these represented. The Scriptures were not something to be debated or questioned. Rather biblical teaching was understood to be that which provided direction to all who walked the road of life.

Thirdly, the inequality of social classes within Victorian society was highly identifiable alongside the prevalent influence of individualism. This stemmed directly from the effects of industrialization which inspired ambition and desire for the good life in so many people. Unfortunately, as individuals sought to get ahead, they became overwhelmed very quickly by the systems in which they had to live and work. As the rich became richer, the poor became poorer and a clear sense of social gap evolved. Not everyone stood in the centre of mainstream religious order. As a result, a very distinct alliance developed between Evangelicals and the working class toward whom they had a special sensitivity and expression of social conscience.

Fourthly, neighbourhood demographics played a significant role because of the way in which people used public space as personal living space. As people opened their windows and doors and gathered readily in the streets, early Salvationist preachers discovered an avenue opened for the hearing of the gospel message. This was a homiletic that went to where the people were. Such openness of community, however, does not represent the landscape of our contemporary neighbourhoods. This difference will warrant our further exploration.

Given this foundation, this interplay between history and homiletic intensifies. Our dialogue now deepens to probe how postmodern/post-Christian voices might respond to this historical summary. Where does the contemporary pulpit find itself alongside the Victorian era? How will we understand the times in which we live in contrast to the times from which an aggressive homiletic emerges? While confrontational preaching found acceptance in a Victorian context, what speed bumps will this form of preaching have to overcome to be helpful to those who stand in today's pulpit?

CHAPTER 4

POSTMODERNISTS COOL TO THE GOSPEL

A T THE TURN OF THE 21ST CENTURY, A WOMAN we will representatively call Michelle (and many others like her) jumps into her SUV at the end of a long day at work, buckles her seat belt and heads home. She plays back her phone messages through her Bluetooth headset as she drives onto the freeway. After a half-hour commute, she punches the code to get into her condominium underground parking lot. Grabbing her sports gear from her workout at the gym and her laptop bag filled with her evening's work, she races to the elevator, again punching her security code. Finally, she arrives at her door. Tossing her bags on the dining room table, she opens the refrigerator, places a frozen dinner in the microwave, presses the message button on her answering machine and grabs the remote control to tune in the evening news. "Two more soldiers lost in conflict as a suicide bomber stormed a military post; the price of gas continues to escalate; homelessness and unemployment statistics are higher than they've ever been and weather patterns continue to predict an unsettled week of severe storms and warnings." All that in just the opening headlines! Later on, Michelle will call her two kids, who are spending the week with their dad. Expecting the arrival of her boyfriend shortly, she reminds herself to get a pregnancy test kit from the drugstore. She hopes that her suspicions are wrong. Looking through the day's mail, she hopes her final divorce papers will soon show up. With all of this lingering, Michelle pulls out a beer from the fridge as she waits for the microwave to finish heating her meal. Guardedly, she stares over at the pile of bills on the desk waiting to be paid. How is anyone supposed to keep up with all this pressure anyway? One day she will get lucky! All she needs is the right set of numbers on her prized lotto ticket or the right string of luck at the casino. Then all her problems will be over! Her mother keeps calling to invite her to church. She says, "Church will solve your problems, Michelle!" But who needs all that religious stuff anyway? As Michelle has been saying for months, "Mom, I've got my truth and you've got yours! I don't need to go to your church to be a good person! Besides, who can really trust what religious people say these days? Too many of them have lost all credibility in my eyes—so what's the point?"

The norms characteristic of a 21st-century postmodern/post-Christian lifestyle are evident in Michelle's story. Consequently, an unrelenting reality confronts the Booths' homiletic. Things are not as they once were. Societal patterns have changed drastically from the days in which early Salvationists first walked the streets of East London. As this confrontation between history and homiletic intensifies, contemporary voices seek to make their claim. Allowing that similarities[1] in both Victorian and contemporary narratives are to be found, particularly as they relate to socio-economic demands and aspirations, the differences also demand a hearing. The key question therefore becomes *what cultural distinctives set the 21st-century mission field apart from the context in which the Booths' homiletic lived and took root?* In order to answer this question, it is necessary to identify what cultural convictions define life as it is known and experienced today. Obviously, Michelle's story is very different from Michael's Victorian narrative. Today's cultural context, separated by space and time, differs substantially from that of people who resided in Victorian times. What insights speak into the truth of this observation?

Postmodern/Post-Christian Connection to Religious Authority

Reality check number one. Today's average person has none; that is to say those living at 21st-century addresses have marginal to non-existent connection with contemporary religious authority and even more so for that which is deemed Christian. If you were to survey a random group of 20- to 30-year-olds, you would very quickly discover how limited the affinity and respect for religious authority is today.[2] Supporting this perspective, Chris Altrock, in *Preaching to Pluralists,* offers a helpful observation when he talks about the spiritual illiteracy of our day. Referencing those born between 1960 and 2000, Altrock concludes that those emerging from this period of history represent a generation with little to no sense of biblical or Christian memory. They have not attended regular Sunday school or worship services with their parents. They do not know the stories, doctrines and vocabulary of the gospel or the larger sense of biblical story.[3] With this lack of background experience and the weighted messages received from media, politics and other varying cultural influences, postmodern/post-Christian pilgrims[4] have come to believe that all truth is relative. Recognizing the need to be socially tolerant and respectful of varying ethnic and religious persuasions, people today have learned to be accepting and open-minded of all expressions of perceived truth. When it comes to discerning truth, the least offensive way and possibly the most logical response is to allow for multiple options. What is true for one may not be true for others. Everyone has a right to their take on truth. The voice of the Church, and more specifically the preacher, is one in a cluttered myriad of cultural messages. Statistics support this claim by suggesting that the average person today takes in over 6,000 different messages every day; what then becomes so special about the gospel?[5] Arguing this point further, *Barna Group Surveys* suggest that most adults in this day and age are more capable of naming the 10 top-rated prime-time television shows than they are able to accurately state the defining theme of the Christian faith.[6] Graham Johnston, in *Preaching to a Postmodern World,* furthers this discussion by asserting that today's preacher can no longer assume preaching takes place within a more or less Christian culture:

> The great narratives of Judeo-Christian belief, the pivotal
> stories of the Bible's characters ... the life and ministry of
> Jesus Christ, either are not known or they do not carry
> the meaning-making significance they did in previous
> generations. People don't need to be given moral
> instruction and Bible stories. The larger challenge is to
> teach how we are to view the world Christianly.[7]

Supporting Johnston's premise, Altrock goes on to qualify that while society today does not have any sense of connection to religious history or biblical story, they are interested in spiritual matters. Unlike their modern counterparts, who embraced science or reason over spiritual issues, postmoderns/post-Christians are highly interested in spirituality.[8] Yet it must be qualified that just because people are interested in spiritual issues does not necessarily mean they are interested in Christian spiritual issues. Altrock argues that there is no better contemporary example of this than the television show *Oprah*:

> In 2002, Oprah Winfrey reached 22 million viewers in 112
> countries.... Its success is surprising given its overt spiritual
> tone. As one article described it, the show "creates
> community, provides information, and encourages people
> to evaluate and improve their lives. *Oprah* consistently
> features an inward focus and challenges viewers to apply
> in their lives, the lessons learned on the show.... In a
> November 2001 show, she stated, "Today, whatever it is
> you believe most deeply, now is the time to embrace it."[9]

Further accentuating this great divide between biblical authority and cultural complacency, societal trends speak to the increasing influence of psychic performers. Such was evident in an article published in *The Winnipeg Free Press,* citing the visit of psychic Sylvia Browne, which over 1,600 people attended. Tickets for this event were $119 to $139 per person. In speaking about the afterlife, Browne alleged that "the soul survives death and the hereafter is not to be feared. It's a beautiful place.... You go with your (spirit) guide to a large temple and view your life and then you decide whether you are going to come back or not."[10] The obvious question emerging from this is whether Browne really has a message about the afterlife, or whether she is simply advancing the possibility that some different version of life continues here on earth. The alarming factor is the manner in which she purports how the individual is able to make the choice and shape this for him or herself. The significant following that Browne and others like her have achieved is deeply troubling to the preacher seeking to have impact for the cause of Christ.

With these examples in view, it is evident that today's society is clearly in search of something, but the ultimate destination is illusive and undefined. Altrock argues that "through prayer, exploration of other religions, through deep interest in the supernatural, people today seek an experience with 'Something or Someone higher then themselves!' "[11] They want to be lifted from a world beyond their own into some better expression of reality. Emphasis toward experience is therefore going to carry much greater weight for individuals rather than a heady explanation of truth. In all of this, it becomes evident that the quest for "something more" no longer takes place via a Christian path, nor does this searching give authoritative credence to the voice of the preacher who seeks to proclaim gospel truths. A prime example of this perspective comes from a recent post-Christian testimony posted online. To those understanding the depth of what this individual has walked away from, the words are cutting to the core.

> I am a former Christian, early 40s, a previous true believer who worshipped mainly in evangelical circles.... I am happy to describe the human being as spiritual, while realizing that this impetus is a phenomenon manufactured within the psyche or society, and not imposed by an external God (especially not the white-bearded guy looking down

from the clouds.) And I am willing to accept the positive, beautiful and poetic elements of *any faith* [emphasis mine] while resisting any attempts by organized religion to impose their dogmas on our (thankfully) secular society.... Christians have no right at all to demand that you respond to their good news. This so called "evidence that demands a verdict" is flimsy hearsay, 2,000 years old at that, and would be thrown out in any court of law.[12]

Into this world, the truth of a disturbing gospel still seeks to be heard and embraced.

These tensions intensify as we consider what Sabbath rest looks like in today's society. While Victorian voices would have argued for the sense of social respectability that church attendance conveyed, today, people are caught up in the ever-increasing busyness of Sunday, which does not frame itself differently from any other day of the week. One can still get to the grocery store or the mall. Life goes on Monday through Sunday without any deviation of pattern; work, rest and play know no boundary of schedule. As a result, the sacredness of Sunday has diminished in both Christian and non-Christian circles, giving further commentary to the manner in which the perceived authority, relevance and necessity of the Church to daily life is becoming more and more a disposable element of culture.

Postmodern/Post-Christian Belief Systems

R eality check number two! It is a new day! Concerns for the afterlife and its rewards and punishments are no longer dominating societal thinking, nor do these theological themes have impact on the way life is lived. In this respect, when confronted with talk about heaven and eternal destination, societal voices say, "So what! Tell me about something that is going to make my life better right here and right now!" Supporting this perspective, Altrock argues that "postmoderns are pragmatic.... They are not interested in life after death—only life before death."[13] Feeding into this reality, the biblical preacher immediately sees the huge disconnect that exists between Victorian and postmodern/post-Christian times. Thoughts of heaven or hell are only of marginal concern, if that at all. Primary interest rests with today and how the bills will be paid; how economic advancement will be achieved or how relationships will be solidified in a sense of present community.[14]

Fueling this perspective further (that is to say the postmodern/post-Christian's preoccupation with present life realities), is the nature of the *therapeutic culture* in which they now live. Robinson and Wall develop this concept effectively in their work *Called to be Church*, as they highlight the manner in which contemporary spirituality now centres itself primarily in the needs of the individual, i.e., "making my life a little better or making me feel better about myself." In this perspective, everything is put in service of self and the result is an "instrumentalizing" of God. Rather than in himself becoming an end or a final destination point, God becomes an instrument toward the human realization of people's own self-centred pre-determined goals.[15]

When we take this perspective to its fullest expression then conversion to Christianity risks a sole motivation of what such a decision might do to improve one's basic quality of life. Robinson and Wall elaborate further, suggesting people would forgive others, not because Christ commanded it, but because it would help them feel better and live longer. People would pray, not because it acknowledges dependency upon God, but because it will soothe troubled nerves and lower our stress levels. Ultimately, life becomes a little bit better for all![16]

> Concerns for the afterlife and its rewards and punishments are no longer dominating societal thinking, nor do these theological themes have impact on the way life is lived

Recognizing the dilemma this stated reality poses, the postmodern/post-Christian perspective pushes a weighted agenda, which requires the biblical preacher to rethink ways in which a predominantly ego-centred society can be helped to hear the passionate claims of the One who says "I AM." Contemporary belief systems, therefore, place the need of the individual at the core of its perspective. The *me* of today is much more important than the *Holy Thee.*

Thirdly, the postmodern/post-Christian thinker truly believes history is out of control. This sits in contrast to Victorian thought that suggested history was evolving directly toward a point of eternal destiny. George G. Hunter, in *How to Reach Secular People* , effectively addresses this idea, pointing to the manner in which world events and natural catastrophes continue to erode public confidence that a better day is coming. People today face the future with great anxiety because they perceive life to be an endless series of large scale shocks, surprises and threats. From "volatile stock markets and oil prices to threats of recessions, unemployment, urban violence, the onslaught of drugs and AIDS epidemic, many people feel that 'no one is in charge.' "[17] Moving from a societal focus that no longer holds religion at the centre of its identity, this sense of hopelessness further increases the inability of people to aspire toward anything better than what they know just now.

A fourth distinction of postmodern/post-Christian thought is the sense in which people are conscious more of personal doubt than they are of personal guilt. Hunter suggests that up until recent times, guilt was a prominent, distinguishing feature of a non-Christian audience. People, he says, were conscious, in days gone by, of personal responsibility and sought the necessary forgiveness where it was appropriate. Today, many people will still acknowledge the guilt that is behind society's problems but now it is someone else's guilt— the 'system, the establishment, their parents' generation, the younger generation.' " Those who would own and identify a profound sense of personal guilt have all but fallen off the radar screen of contemporary society.[18]

Barbara Brown Taylor reinforces this perspective as she speaks to the difficulty of trying to convince people of their sinful condition:

> Try telling someone who's been disciplined by advertising
> that he is a sinner? A hundred years ago, a preacher
> would have seen heads nod in recognition at that familiar
> concept. But today's consumer is likely to be shocked—
> baffled. How could he be a sinner? All he knows is that he
> is unhappy because he does not have his fair share of stuff

and he isn't appreciated enough by those around him.[19]

It is in light of this reality that today's 21st-century preacher is going to have a significantly more difficult time proclaiming the demanding claims of the gospel, particularly since salvation requires an acknowledgement of personal guilt and a desire to turn from wrongdoing. Before the preacher attempts to scale the heights of this message, it is advisable for him or her to take note that an air of resistance is already looming before a word even leaves the pulpit.

Breakdown of Social Classes

While evangelical dissenters within Victorian England identified where the social gap was in terms of religious involvement, our society today may struggle to define such a clear-cut picture. Today's preacher is challenged to call up the roll on a Sunday morning to identify who is absent from the worship event. Which societal class is missing from our pews? Does our faith community represent the true demographic of our neighbourhood? As we engage this conversation, we discover very quickly that people from all stations of life have become distant and disenfranchised from organized religion. While in the Victorian age, the rich demonstrated their social respectability by disciplined observance of the Sabbath, this focus no longer defines our cultural landscape. In the Booths' day it was the impoverished that were not finding their way into the churches. Sadly, today, people from all stations of life have become disinterested and distant to religious expression. We can no longer say our primary mandate is to get the gospel to the poor, although it remains central to what we are about as a Salvation Army. Rather we need to think about how the claims of a disturbing gospel will reach all people in all places. Clarifying the profile of our audience is critical to our task. Knowing our audience is essential. The Christian Church has to work much harder now to be an influential voice that impacts social behaviour and the choices people make. Don Posterski invites preachers to recognize how in the eyes of culture, "God used to be our hero, the star player in the starting line up. Today we have relegated him to the reserves. He sits on the bench as a second stringer. It is only in certain circumstances we may bring him off the bench to enter the game" and this is only if God is deemed to have any sense of contemporary relevance to our world.[20] Given the reality of our current context, preachers need to rethink why their churches are not attracting all demographics of society. This includes the rich, the poor and everyone else in between. Interestingly, the *Barna Group Surveys* suggests the number one reason people give for not going to church is "I am too busy." Barna translates that to mean "... really they believe that the church has nothing to offer them. They believe their lifestyles to be incompatible with the expectations of the church."[21] The two testimonials that follow speak further into the void perceived by those living in a postmodern/post-Christian context, particularly as it relates to the relevance of church to their lives:

> The Christian Church has to work much harder now to be an influential voice that impacts social behaviour and the choices people make

I got tired of hearing sermons about being nice to people, or how important it is to read the Bible or give money to the church so they could bring in more people who could be told to be nice to other people and read the Bible.

I've got three kids at home who don't have nice clothing, who don't get a vacation trip every year, who have never been to Disney World. They don't see much of me or their dad because we're working ourselves silly to make ends meet. Sure it's great to be nice to your neighbours and to understand when others mistreat you. But that's not the problem in my life. I am tired, lonely, on the edge financially, and I don't see any light at the end of my tunnel. I don't really care about choirs, short-term missions trips, youth-group events or men's breakfast groups. I'm drowning in the whirlpool of life's realities. The church isn't helping me. And like they say, if it ain't part of the solution, then it must be part of the problem.[22]

Clearly, the challenges become more pronounced as this interplay between history and homiletic evolves.

Changing Neighbourhood Demographics

We would have to travel quite a distance in the world-wide context to find neighbourhood streets which would offer an exact mirroring of the Victorian era. Certainly, in the North American context, people primarily live behind closed doors. Windows remain closed because of air conditioning or the possibility of vandalism or robbery. Children do not play openly in the streets, not only because of traffic concerns but also for fear of child abductions. People, in most cases, do not know who their neighbours are. Although this may be qualified in some smaller rural/tribal settings, in larger suburban and metropolitan centres the impact of this distinguishing factor is huge. Robert Wuthnow in *After the Baby Boomers* assists in further explaining this current phenomenon, citing the manner in which adults isolate themselves from each other:

> A married woman in her early 30s says *Bowling Alone* definitely describes life in her middle-class suburb. "We get in our car and go to Wal-Mart or to work. We're so segmented. We don't see our neighbours. We don't even have a five-minute meaningful conversation with folks.... I didn't even realize our next-door neighbours went to our church.... We'd been there almost three years before we met them.[23]

This sense of isolation in community is accentuated as we identify the difficulty we will have in finding ways to penetrate the closed nature of our neighbourhoods. Any expression of open-air ministry is going to require civic permission. Add to this the significant challenges in securing an audience; community life does not extend itself readily to open public spaces. While we may see some activity at the local basketball court or on the community centre ice rink, the kind of activity once found in the streets and the openness of homes in the Victorian context is quite a disconnect from where people live today. Society has become more of a "closed neighbourhood," caught up primarily in what happens within ones' individual home. An increased sense of guardedness prevails. Who can be truly trusted? What is desirable to bring into the home? What should we leave out on the front step? At least in the sense of community we build online, we can choose when to log on and when to log off. We can delete friends and block contact. The big point here is that today's preacher navigates a complex cultural divide, where community has redefined itself as closed, guarded and completely overrun by its busyness. Into this context the preacher is still required to present the forthright claims of *a disturbing gospel*; i.e. you must be born again; true life is only found through Jesus Christ; surrender yourself to him! How shall the preacher help people hear this Word as life-giving and true? What can the preacher do to assist listeners in seeing this disturbing gospel message as one that has the power to transport them from the reality defined into something that truly is transformative and renewing? What can be *disturbed* in the present, in order to improve the prognosis of the future? It is in this respect that we seek application of a post-Booth homiletic, where the strengths of the Booths' early approach to preaching integrate with the challenges of today's pulpit.

Summary

As this historical/homiletical interplay comes to a moment of pause, new assertions become evident as postmodern/post-Christian voices make their striking claims:

1. We are a society no longer connected to biblical story.

2. We are a society that no longer values the authoritative voice of the Church; we have our own brand of truth.

3. We are more interested in life before death versus life after death; our primary concern is therapeutic; making life better now.

4. We believe that history is out of control; no one is in charge.

5. We are a society more easily given to doubt than a people who will acknowledge our own guilt. Bottom line— someone else is to blame but not us.

6. We are redefining breakdown of social class—it is not only the poor of our society that are sitting on the fringes of religion. Churches need to figure out why they are not appealing to everyone right across the board!

7. Our sense of safe public space has changed. We live in closed neighbourhoods.

With these lines clearly drawn, the task remains to name the specific challenges and tensions that are evolving from that which is represented by both Victorian and contemporary voices. Restating our common ground—we still have a sin problem! What is to be ultimately gained from this juxtaposition of history and homiletic and how does a concise rendering of the issues raised assist preachers in moving forward to speak into the homiletical challenges of the day?

Naming the Evolving Questions

While sometimes both a challenging and painful process, to sit back and evaluate what is true about the times in which we live is a necessary exercise. As we do this, we hear the sidebar conversation between a historical and a contemporary homiletic. To preachers of the Booths' time, those of the postmodern/post-Christian era freely say, "Of course your way of doing it worked! Society was already on the page you were representing—people were already speaking your language; they were well familiar with the story you told. Not so in our time and space." Counteracting this perspective, the Booths' homiletic reminds us that the truths of the gospel remain the same. Sin is still sin and remains the overriding problem bringing brokenness to our world. We do not rewrite Scripture just because our social context has changed. The preacher still has a mandate to proclaim all of God's truth. Recognizing these tensions, key questions arise, inviting further thought and reflection:

1. How shall people be persuaded toward biblical truth when there is a present lack of relationship and respect toward the institution of the Church itself?

2. How is the preacher to regain credibility, to be heard by the 21st-century listener as one who has a valuable and necessary message to bring?

3. How are the themes of heaven and hell to be preached when, according to the postmodern/post-Christian thinker, these terms have no defining value or morally persuasive power to impact contemporary society? Should these topics of preaching now become obsolete?

4. Is it possible to address the widening audience postmodern/post-Christian thinkers represent in terms of those who are sitting on the fringes of the community of faith? Is the Booths' approach to preaching solely for the downtrodden and disenfranchised of society? How do preachers determine the gap into which they should now preach?

5. Given the current cultural landscape, does confrontational preaching still have a place in biblical proclamation or is this approach simply too intrusive and aggressive for today's listener to embrace?

Adding the Voice of Contemporary Salvationists

While the questions previously stated speak to the main challenges of aligning a post-Booth homiletic into the contemporary preaching landscape, it is worthwhile to consider the impact of removing the historical voice from this conversation for a moment. Let us bring in the voices of those who currently preach in Salvation Army circles, to assess whether this brings any new questions or observations. To facilitate this inclusion, 30 sermons were reviewed from Salvation Army preachers across the Canada and Bermuda Territory. Each of these submissions came from preachers in varying ministry contexts, including frontline inner-city missions, suburban congregations on a small, medium and large scale, rural settings, and from preachers who serve in contexts where their primary function is administrative oversight to the larger organization.

Insights are drawn only from what comes from the written page—what might be added or enhanced through the actual preaching event is lost to the reader of the sermon's text for obvious reasons. Also, the sermon samples are not guaranteed to be a representative selection and cannot give a comprehensive view of each preacher's larger commitment to the proclamation of biblical canon. With these qualifying statements identified, we ask what is true about the use of a Salvation Army (Booth) homiletic in the contemporary context? Is the homiletic of William and Catherine Booth still in existence? According to previously identified criteria, is current preaching demonstrating evidence of aggression or urgency of the gospel message? Is simplicity of approach, creativity, relevance to culture and the ultimate validation of truth through personal experience finding a place in the Salvationist pulpit? Do we sense in the contemporary preacher's voice a burden for lost souls? What is currently being presented in

> Sin is still sin and remains the overriding problem bringing brokenness to our world. We do not rewrite Scripture just because our social context has changed

our pulpits? How might this assessment further assist today's preacher in understanding the challenges of proclaiming a disturbing gospel?

Most of the sermons reviewed represented at least some reflection of characteristics defining an early Booth homiletic. Language of culture was readily found, and in many instances, simplicity of approach was evident through the use of conversational writing style. Strength is also noted in the attempt of sermons to make strong claims about the power of the gospel message to change human lives. Approximately 50 percent of reviewed material would fall into this category. In the area of creativity, approximately 20 percent (mostly younger preachers) incorporated video clips. Others used interesting life stories to bring a fresh take to the stated biblical theme. In addition to this, out of all sermons viewed, eight percent emphasized the unique calling of the Salvationist and the distinct mission owned to serve suffering humanity. While it is not always possible for a single sermon to draw all these distinguishing characteristics together into one expression of preaching, we can say that in general Salvationist preachers are working hard to honour the preaching tradition from which they have come.

Some further observations, however, merit documentation. Firstly, it is evident that those who work most closely to the Booths' original cultural context, i.e., the working-class poor, would seem to be the voices that most directly represent the early Salvation Army homiletic, but in a toned-down approach. Simply stated, there is no language found that suggests the goal is to "annihilate the excuses of the sinner!"[24] Nor is the message one that is spoken confrontationally. What is identified are sermons that clearly speak about the difference Christ makes in the life of a believer and the need to accept God's gift of grace through the cross of Calvary. The focus of this theme is not so easily found in samples of sermons received from suburban contexts, where one assumes the preacher, through texts chosen, is addressing those who have been on the road of faith for some time.

Secondly, the form and style of preaching encountered clearly reflects when homiletical training took place. Those who trained in earlier schools of homiletical thought, i.e., approximately 1965-1989, would still organize preaching ideas propositionally and subdivide main ideas and supporting ideas within the sermon body. Those more recently trained (post 1990) have adopted more of a narrative approach, with the intent of getting primarily at big ideas. Often, however, regardless of sermonic form utilized, the centrality of biblical text was sometimes overshadowed by topical treatments of varying themes. This happened as preachers worked in different ways to get at the heartbeat of human struggle. Finding the means to balance these perspectives remains one of the central challenges all preachers face in the preaching task.

Thirdly, it is evident from the sermon samplings that much of current Salvation Army preaching seeks to say a great deal about texts, the ultimate goal being explanation. While this could be perceived as a positive in terms of honouring biblical content, it does very little to create experiences of biblical story, for which today's listeners long. By that I mean, it is not enough to give information about the text and to explain theological content. Today's congregants want to engage the text on their own terms; they want to attend the biblical event, they do not want the preacher to just report about it. Too often, our preaching has failed to acknowledge this need. The preacher takes the trip into the biblical text on behalf of the listener and instead of inviting him or her to get on the next tour bus leaving the station so they can experience it for themselves,

Today's congregants want to engage the text on their own terms; they want to attend the biblical event, they do not want the preacher to just report about it

they say, "Let me tell you what all this means." Usually this follows with a second move which says, "This is how all this applies to our lives." While this is a faithful and true way of expounding on Scripture, the listener will often miss the tension and the struggle of the text and the ultimate sense of victory that can come because they were just being told "about the text." The real goal is to get listeners inside the text where they can experience the truth and the weightiness of the text for themselves. While more will be said about this in a later chapter, we understand the tendency within sermons sampled to take a more informational versus experiential approach to preaching. It is in this respect that the spirit of an early Booth homiletic may struggle to find its voice.

With this commentary offered, what then seems to be missing in the sermon samples reviewed? Interestingly, not one of the sermons had any direct mention of heaven, hell, eternal judgment or guilt as it relates to personal sin. Not one of the sermons directly invited listeners to think about matters of eternal importance or the need for a personal ordering of priorities given the temporal nature of our earthly existence. While this is not meant to be a condemning word to those who have written these sermons or to those who may write similar sermons, the observation validates the challenge that is before us. As Salvationist preachers speak into the moment in the way they best know how, they are continually having to navigate what it means to be culturally sensitive and respectful of the audiences to which they preach. It could be suggested that caution is being exercised, recognizing the air of resistance that may already be registering. This observation, however, raises an important question. Should the themes of a disturbing gospel be completely eliminated from biblical preaching, because it is recognized that it may not

> Should the themes of a disturbing gospel be completely eliminated from biblical preaching, because it is recognized that it may not be a popular message?

be a popular message? If it does not show up directly in a sermon, through the voice of a preacher, where is it people today will be challenged to think of these matters? Can one responsibly preach the full breadth of Scripture and avoid these theological themes altogether? Perhaps more importantly, instead of thinking what preaching about heaven and hell takes away from the preaching moment, what might it add? How might a treatment of the gospel's good news be further enhanced by our deliberate attention to the hard claims of Scripture, particularly as it relates to the judgment and wrath of God? To this tension, we turn our attention in the next chapter.

Finally, it must be noted that the perceived energy and passion of an early Booth homiletic, readily identified in the written forms of historical sermons, struggles to find a mirroring reflection in contemporary works. It could be argued that energy and passion are conveyed only through the uniqueness of personality or through the moment of spoken proclamation, where tone is heard and body language is seen. However, when written copies of the Booths' sermons are placed alongside our own contemporary efforts, we have no difficulty in identifying the Booths' urgency of conviction and passionate belief in the truth of the message. For the Booths, there was an earnest desire that the good news of the text would get inside the person in ways that would truly change the listener's outlook on life. This presses the argument that what is observed in this form of preaching is not about strategy or creative communication theory. Rather, that which was inside the preacher found an outward expression filled with vitality, energy and life. Ironically, in the case of the early Booth homiletic, this was successful in reaching today's historical reader even through the printed page.

In response, we ask what is happening inside the mind and the heart of today's preacher to inspire passionate proclamation? First and foremost, preaching will always be about the deep work of the Spirit. Words for proclamation arise from experiences where the preacher brings himself or herself close to a holy flame. In this sacred place, the Spirit ignites a word of revelation that will not be subdued until it has reached prophetic utterance. In this regard, we cannot assume preaching is only about the navigation of the cultural and contextual challenges we have identified. It is not only about embracing the weight and the difficulty of the message.

> Preaching will always be about the deep work of the Spirit. Words for proclamation arise from experiences where the preacher brings himself or herself close to a holy flame

We must consider what barriers we, ourselves, as preachers place in the way of our proclamation. Given all of life's distractions and responsibilities, how close are we living to the flame of the Spirit, so that holy fire ignites in our preaching? How does the preacher's own spiritual formation assist in creating an expectation of divine event-fulness; so much so that we truly expect God will show up when we rise to the preaching moment? If we address these tensions, we move closer to uncovering how contemporary preachers present the disturbing claims of the gospel with confidence and blessed assurance.

Conclusion

Where have we been and where are we going? Lest this intersecting between history and homiletic seem a directionless journey, the following is offered by means of overall summary.

As the Booth homiletic found its footing in Victorian England, there were certain cultural conditions that facilitated its acceptance and success.

1. A sense of religious authority was generally tolerated in Victorian England. This applied not only to the Church but more specifically to the office of the clergy. Culturally speaking, the voice of the preacher had something valuable to bring to society.

2. Victorian England was centred in the norms of religious life; this impacted not only personal belief systems but patterns of behaviour.

3. Preaching spoke into a cultural gap; the working poor, by nature of their dismal circumstances, were especially open to embrace the message that was being presented to them.

Postmodern/post-Christian voices respond with some initial agreement. Sin is still the dominating problem uniting both the historical and contemporary worlds. Yet people today live at new cultural addresses that would be foreign to the world William and

Catherine Booth knew.

1. Postmodern/post-Christian listeners have no connection to the biblical story, and religious authority has lost its impact and primacy of influence.

2. Postmodern/post-Christians listeners are more interested in life before death versus life after death. Their key concern is to make life better now!

3. Postmodern/post-Christian listeners believe history is out of control.

4. Postmodern/post-Christians listeners are more centred in personal doubt than personal guilt.

5. The postmodern/post-Christian audience has been redefined. The poor are not the only ones sitting on the fringes of religious circles.

6. Postmodern/post-Christian listeners now live in closed neighbourhoods.

To these challenges, key questions invite further exploration.

1. How shall people today connect to the truths of Scripture if there is already a defined disconnect between the secular world and the authority of the Church?

2. Into this setting, how is the preacher to regain a voice that has the power to impact and persuade listeners to one prescribed expression of truth: "Jesus Christ—the way, the truth and the life"?

3. Does the contemporary preacher simply abandon the hard claims of the gospel as it relates to God's judgment and wrath? What is missed if we take this piece out of proclamation? What is gained if it is included? What is the best means for this to be accomplished?

4. What most personally challenges today's preacher as it relates to application of the Booth homiletic? What formative work is required, spiritually speaking, to assist

the preacher in not only preaching the hard claims of a disturbing gospel, but to do this in a way that is motivating and inspirational?

5. Ultimately what does the Booths' approach to preaching offer that will assist the contemporary preacher? What needs to be set aside? What elements require a re-contextualizing in order to address the complexities of today's preaching task?

It is in the naming of these questions that a call is given for this historical-homiletical intersecting to resume. The desired outcome is to embrace deeper insights into the challenges of contemporary preaching, and how *proclaiming a disturbing gospel* is not only possible, but a needful part of the way in which the Church will be required to define its preaching ministry, beyond this present time and space.

CHAPTER 5

REKINDLING THE FLAME

W INSTON FLETCHER PARODIED A CONTEMPORARY preaching event by imagining the way in which 37 present-day British cathedrals might be improved:

> Sermons should be drafted centrally and distributed by fax. And they should be interactive. Each member of the congregation should have a remote control console with a red button to press when bored. More than 50 percent press their buttons and a red light shines in the pulpit warning the preacher to get on with it. Three reds and he's out. Soon every pew would have its own mini TV, networked so that cathedral-goers can choose which of the 37 services on offer look the most heavenly. Soon costs would be veritably slashed with one of the best two or three services serving all 37 cathedrals.[1]

While much could be said about this particular interpretation of preaching, what is clearly represented is the mindset of secular society that demands a certain entertainment value in the pulpit. This playful parody assumes a boredom factor will quickly set in and congregants will become disengaged from the preaching event. What if we imagined new possibilities? What if people were lining up outside the doors of our churches, as if we were about to release the next premiere of Hollywood's latest blockbuster movie? What if people came early to our congregations, to make sure they had a good seat for the sermon? What if people were walking away from the Sunday service saying, "I can't wait to see what next week's message is going to be about"? What if people were talking about their new insights into God's truth? What if this experience was changing how people interacted in their homes and workplace? What if society was becoming a better place to live because of the impact of persuasive biblical preaching? What if there were fewer break-in robbery reports, fewer instances of abuse, fewer people needing rehabilitation programs, less homelessness and hunger in our city streets, and fewer people lining up for assistance in our social services centres? What if more employers were caring about employees, more teachers caring about the needs of students and more doctors caring about their patients? What if people were taking their Sunday morning experience out into the streets of their community, and their neighbours were readily noticing that something was changing, that something seemed to be vastly different about the person they had known and the person now standing before them? What if Christian communities were identified like the early Church, as places that were "daily adding to their number" (Acts 2:47)? What if society was all of a sudden feeling at home in the company of God's people?

"Believe again you have a message that truly can make a difference for the days in which you live!" In the words of Catherine Booth, "Preacher; don't be afraid to disturb the present, in order that you might be able to improve the future"

Such was both the vision and the spirit of the early homiletic of The Salvation Army, captured by the Movement's first preachers, William and Catherine Booth. Such is the vision now needed as contemporary preachers seek to convince secular society of its need to wake up to the truths of God, and to see how these truths have relevance in our world today. The great homiletical call now blaring its way into the preacher's ear is "Believe again you have a message that truly can make a difference for the days in which you live!" In the words of Catherine Booth, "Preacher; don't be afraid to disturb the present, in order that you might be able to improve the future."[2]

Using the foundational principles of the Booth homiletic identified thus far as a primary point of reference, what is needed to achieve this outcome? Otherwise stated, what is required to effectively assimilate the Booth homiletic[3] with that which has been described as a postmodern/post-Christian landscape? In this chapter, consideration will be given to elements that assist in persuading postmodern/post-Christian listeners to embrace a difficult and disturbing gospel. Support will also be offered from varying sources to demonstrate the way in which this homiletic is already speaking to the challenges of the contemporary pulpit. Many of the issues faced today in our pulpits are not new. In particular, the Booth homiletic transcends historical space and offers wisdom for today. Where the specific strategies of the Booths may no longer apply, the spirit of this homiletic has much to say about the manner in which preaching may now be engaged.

Fire Starter One: Offering Something New

God could offer suffering humanity a new reality. Likewise, people today seek a new reality; they want their worlds to be reframed into something more hopeful than what they now know.

"We are engaged in making a new people." Such was the claim of William Booth in a sermon he delivered at a Staff Officers Councils, and this was subsequently published in *The Staff Review*, April 1924.[4] Drawing thematically from the life story of Moses, the Founder worked the primary idea: "Moses got his people out of Egypt. You have to do the same. He kept them from going back. You can do the same."[5] What emerges as most striking in this quotation is the manner in which early Salvation Army homiletical thought recognized the opportunity preaching presented to lift people from their current reality into something new. Catherine Booth reinforced this premise in her sermon "Adaptation of Measures," and demonstrated the method through which this was to be done:

> If this be the case, WHAT IS TO BE DONE? What would strike you should be done in the state of comparative—spiritual eclipse? Evidently it would be madness to *go on as we are*. That will mend nothing. Somebody must strike and do something worthy of the emergency. There is no improving the future, without disturbing the present.... We are so conservative by nature—especially some of us. We have such a rooted dislike to have anything rooted up, disturbed or knocked down. It is as much the work of God, however, to "knock down and pull up and to destroy" as to build up, and God's ambassadors frequently have to do as much of one as the other.[6]

... the need for counter-cultural preaching is the most urgent mandate of our day

Clearly from Catherine's exhortation, there is a deep sense in which preaching was to direct its energies toward a vision of transformation. "We cannot go on as we are!" In the "knocking down, pulling up, destroying and building up," a significant spiritual work was being done. A new kingdom reality was being created. Capturing something more of this emphasis in contemporary terms, David Lose, in *Confessing Jesus Christ*, articulates the process through which preachers work to create new possibilities for their listeners. In so doing, the importance of disclosing and articulating truths relative to the present nature of human existence is identified. This becomes linked with "the act of bringing new reality into being, an act of creation.... It is an act of redeeming and transforming reality, an act of shattering illusions and cracking open limited perspectives ... an invitation to build a profoundly different world.[7]

In this respect, the need for counter-cultural preaching is the most urgent mandate of our day. Today's preacher cannot be content to tell people—those who are Christians and those who are not—what they most want to hear. The great need of congregations today is to tell people what they need to hear in order that their lives would "not go on as they are!" The goal is that preaching would lead listeners into a new spiritual reality that is defined by a personal experience of God's love and grace. Numerous voices in the current homiletical community echo this theme as preachers are waking up to the richness of opportunity to counteract and counter-balance the limited perspectives of secular society. Michael Quicke, in *360 Degree Preaching*, validates this premise:

> In too many places, preaching has been reduced to an anemic, religious non-event. Faint is its power to proclaim an alternative reality, the kingdom of God, and faded is its conviction about transforming communities. Gone are its prophetic voices and its mission thrust. Missing is its subversive way of challenging the status quo to create communities of light and service.... Preachers have lost the art of leadership through the proclaimed Word. There is too little courage and too much safe predictability, too little confrontation of evil by Christ's power and too much soothing of the already convinced.[8]

Does this now mean that the preacher rises to the pulpit this Sunday to tell it like it is, to straighten people out once and for all and to make sure they get their acts together spiritually speaking? No. Given the guardedness to which postmodern/post-Christian listeners may come to the preaching event and the manner in which connection to biblical authority is already strained, a different approach is needed. The Booth homiletic, now projecting relevance to contemporary expression, can no longer rest on the merits of finger-pointing, guns-loaded, sock-it-to-them kind of preaching. Rather the *"you need to; we need to"* imperatives of preaching now need to be balanced with a stronger assertion of *"you can—we can"* claims, which ultimately point to the salvific power of God to breathe new life into old wineskins. Taking this point further, preaching aspires to proclaim: *"You can* know release from your fears; *you can* know joy in your sadness; *you can* know peace in your troubles! Why? Because

God's grace is within your reach! God speaks his truth when he says, "Fear not, I am with you!" (Psalm 46:1-2), "In your sufferings, I will fill you with an inexpressible, glorious joy!" (1 Peter 1:8), "Take hope, I will keep you in perfect peace, if you focus everything completely on me" (Isaiah 26:3). Quicke argues this point further when he suggests that "preaching is nothing less than sharing the in-breaking of God's good news to create new people in a new community."[9] Noted theologian and scholar Walter Brueggemann further frames this in a manner that assists the preacher in realizing the true potential of what preaching can achieve: "[Preaching] is the evoking of an alternative community that knows it is about different things in different ways."[10] To assist the reader in unpacking the significance of this insight, Quicke offers the following as summary:

> When Jesus Christ came proclaiming (Mark 1:14), his primary concern was not to impart new information but to announce a new way of living in his kingdom. "Repent and believe in the good news." This is not a tinkering with life as we know it but an invitation to a new way of being never imagined before. It is not a dabbling with surface issues of passing significance but a dealing at depth with our reasons for existence in his kingdom—issues of eternal consequence.[11]

We can imagine William and Catherine Booth somewhere on heaven's balcony echoing an "amen" to these convictions. The vision of something new—something better than what is known right now—is that which has the potential to capture the attention of today's complacent pew sitter. This will only happen effectively, however, as the hard claims of the gospel are put in direct conversation with God's redemptive action in our world. This will mean putting difficult gospel claims in dialogue with God's saving work in the past (affirming divine credibility), in the present (affirming divine relevancy) and in the future (affirming divine dependability). This process further illuminates the nature of the hermeneutical task of the preacher and the importance of actively engaging the whole text to capture what is alive and active within it. Robinson and Wall reinforce this perspective, in *Called to Be Church,* as they urge biblical preachers to discover how scriptural narrative engages and draws people in, reframing a new vision of the world and of the Church. Citing an analogy offered by biblical scholar J. Louis Martyn, a helpful picture emerges as to what postmodern/post-Christian preaching is really all about. Martyn had imagined a team of students and archeologists diligently working away on some dry dusty dig to uncover an especially well-preserved mummy. One thing was for certain in this process—the subject they sought was dead, without life and sustenance. Imagine their surprise when the mummy suddenly leapt up, grabbed a spade from the nearest scientist and hit him over the head with it.[12] Now imagine this reality in the contemporary pulpit—perceived dead things coming to life and those making the find impacted in tangible, heartfelt ways?

The words of the writer to the Hebrews press a timely and relevant emphasis: "For the Word of God is living and active. Sharper than any double-edged sword, it penetrates even dividing soul and spirit, joints and marrow" (Hebrews 4:12). Such was the conviction that shaped and defined the early preaching of The Salvation Army. Guided by the belief that Scripture was a living thing, William and Catherine Booth maintained throughout their ministry that this Word had the power to reframe new visions of what life could be; in both the temporal and eternal perspectives. Contemporary preachers will need new homiletical skills to reframe the familiar stories of Scripture and present them in ways that are fresh and engaging.

Recognizing the challenges now raised, the preacher is encouraged to think about new ways to creatively engage biblical texts for preaching. To begin this journey, it is helpful to initially think about what contemporary images connect to the original setting of the biblical text. In developing this creativity, note that this is about more than sermons supported by the creative inclusion of technology, PowerPoint slides and video clips. Today's preacher is challenged to become an artist with images that are created through the power of words. To reach these places of homiletical breakthrough, preachers themselves will need to enter into playful and imaginative encounters with their texts. For example, what would it have looked like to have sat in the boat with the disciples and to have felt the pain of straining at the oars against the prevailing winds (Mark 6:45-56)?

What kind of conversation would have taken place? e.g., *"I don't know, boys, if I can keep this up much longer. My arms are just about to give out! What were we thinking when we decided to come out here tonight? How will we ever make it back to shore?"* Furthermore, what if the action in the story had not played out the way the biblical writer narrates? Imagine if Jesus had just kept on walking past the disciples, as the text indicated he intended to do (Mark 6:48). Imagine the possible response of the disciples if in fact they had identified the ghostly form before them as Jesus. But in actual fact as they became aware of a stranger on the sea, they did not recognize their Lord. Herein, Mark opens a window for us to see the way in which the disciples struggled to understand the lessons Jesus was teaching. By looking for alternate versions of the screenplay (i.e. the way the movie does not get scripted) preachers are led closer to the power of the way in which the story is told. Jesus does not ignore his disciples struggling against the wind. Jesus does not give up on his followers because they are incredibly slow learners! But Jesus gets into the boat. In this story, we see a powerful picture of the persistence of grace, and the manner in which Jesus draws near to his struggling disciples—even when they fail to recognize him. As the Word is imaginatively encountered, historical distance is bridged by a sense of new life emerging from the written page. Listeners are then invited to sit in a new place within the text. They are encouraged to see new pictures of who Jesus is and the new realities that can be realized as a result of this sacred encounter.[13] Marva Dawn, in *Unfettered Hope*, offers perhaps the best closing word on this matter:

> In a world of techno-sophistication that daily erodes the last vestiges of wonder in ordinary life, hungry souls yearn for a message from God. The mandate of the preacher is to live with such integrity in the presence of God and to study the Word with such energy and giftedness that when he or she finally stands to speak, those who listen will experience an in-breaking of the invisible world that literally *brings their frantic lives to a stop* [emphasis mine] and sends them away transformed by their response to the gospel.[14]

Believing in the truth of this assertion, preachers are invited to think more specifically about what *stop signs* each Sunday morning sermon is holding up for congregants, what is being presented that truly arrests the attention of the listeners and ultimately leads them to say, "There's something fresh in that Word today!"

Fire Starter Two: A Need to Wake Up Sleeping Sinners

The early preachers of The Salvation Army believed they had an aggressive work to do to wake up sleeping sinners to fullness of life in Christ. Preaching is still about getting the attention of the people and pointing them to Jesus Christ.

As has been identified throughout this work, one of the most difficult elements to negotiate around the re-contextualization of the Booth homiletic is the anticipated manner in which confrontational preaching will be received. Recognizing that the word *confrontation* in itself often denotes hostile engagement of opposing forces, the challenge is to seek what the full connotation of this term can mean, as applied to the preaching task. Is confrontational preaching only to be understood as a negative or is there some intrinsic value represented as preachers challenge listeners to come face to face with the reality of their spiritual condition and how this impacts their eternal destiny? Eddie Gibbs, in *Church Next*, offers significant insight as to both the strengths and weaknesses of confrontational preaching. Arguing in a positive light, Gibbs suggests that confrontational preaching responds to a conviction that "as many as possible should hear as soon as possible, as clearly as possible."[15] While mission values and urgency press this agenda forward, postmodern/ post-Christian listeners would argue that at times this form of preaching seems overbearing and intrusive. Particularly in the West, people are resistant to unsolicited approaches and feel that they already know enough about the Church and its message. They have come to consider Christianity to be irrelevant, intrusive, insensitive and intolerant of other faith traditions. "Once people have been scarred by such a confrontation, it is all the more difficult to gain a considerable hearing.[16]

If this is truly an accurate representation of the postmodern/ post-Christian barometer as it relates to openness to gospel proclamation, then contemporary preachers find themselves at an interesting crossroad. The urgent message of the gospel, "now is the time of salvation," linked with the imperative call which says "all must be born again," now creates a major road obstruction. The question confronting us is whether or not we should remove this obstruction altogether. Do we simply say it is no longer important, or is there a way to honour the integrity of this gospel claim in a way that will engage those who sit before the preacher Sunday after Sunday? It is this latter position that is held up in this work as the most desirable. How can this be achieved? Drawing from a range of current homiletical thinking in this area, we find four resolves that help us answer this question and show us how it is possible for a Booth homiletic to meet the challenges of this present age.

Firstly, if people are going to grasp the demanding claims of the gospel, they must be invited gradually and respectfully into this conversation. Adam Hamilton, in *Unleashing the Word*, argues that "the best way to influence and persuade others is not to alienate and irritate them but to honour them and respect their positions, and then to respectfully and humbly offer an alternative position."[17] While in this perspective there is a danger of losing the ability to truly be counter-cultural in that the preacher will need to say "... I hear what you are saying; I see your perspective," the key is that the second part of Hamilton's equation is realized—that an alternative position is truly represented. Herein, significant skill is needed to speak apologetically into the theological tensions of the day, along with ability to effectively engage in these conversations. The desired outcome is that those outside the context of the Christian community are given an opportunity to engage the claims of Christian faith in the hope that this will lead to an awakening experience of faith.

Secondly, if the hard claims of the gospel are going to be heard and embraced in a contemporary setting, listeners will require the ability to see how their story connects to God's story. David Lose, in

Confessing Jesus Christ, frames this in a helpful way when he suggests the importance of preaching that "persuades experience to meet the text while simultaneously seeking the text to meet experience."[18] In other words, the challenge of the preacher is to facilitate a meeting place through which the text intersects with the life of the listener. As preachers attempt to do this in their sermons, we cannot help but hear the recurring theme of the Booth homiletic. William and Catherine Booth exemplified consistently in their preaching that their goal was to make the Scripture relevant to ordinary life. The vision was that listeners would find a mirrored reflection of their own pain and struggle within God's Word and that this fresh insight would lead them toward their deliverance and healing. In this respect, today's listeners will only respond to preaching that is perceived to be speaking into the questions of the day.

Alongside this, preachers will need to acknowledge both the obvious and less obvious questions a biblical text raises. For example, why does a forgiving, merciful God strike a husband and wife dead for holding back a portion of their tithe (see Acts 5:1-11)? Why does Jesus refuse candidates for discipleship last opportunities to go home and bury their dead, or to at least say good-bye to their families (see Luke 9:57-62)? If Jesus is interested in effective candidate recruitment, surely this approach seems devoid of human sensitivity. Consider the story of Isaiah's dramatic encounter with the Lord's presence in the Temple (Isaiah 6:1-13). After moments of intense worship and personal cleansing, Isaiah receives a commission to a ministry that appears doomed to failure from the start. People will be "ever hearing, but never understanding, ever seeing but never perceiving" (vs. 9). Someone, somewhere in the wings has to be asking, "What is the point in this?" Today's preacher will achieve a much stronger connection between the pulpit and the pew by leaning hard into the questions that texts raise for listeners. Where are the speed bumps? What makes it difficult to steer the course of a text? New pulpit energy will be found as listeners set out on an investigative journey with the preacher to resolve textual tensions and questions.

Supporting this emphasis, William Willimon, in *The Intrusive Word,* argues that before the gospel can become an answer to our deepest longings, first it must become a question. Otherwise stated, "within the gospel's answer is the provocation of our most perplexing questions. If this be God, in the presence of this Jew from Nazareth, then who are we? How then shall we live? What is going on in our world?"[19] Understanding the progression of this overall process becomes essential to the preacher finding his or her way from text to sermon.

Building further upon these convictions, a re-contextualization of the Booths' homiletic will require an emphasis toward *creating experiences* of biblical texts, rather than sermons that focus on lengthy explanations of theological themes. It is only as listeners are able to enter into the sacred place of the Word, with their own flashlights aimed toward the path, that they will be able to identify where their story connects with God's story. In this respect, congregants likely will require help breathing in the fragrant air of Eden's garden, to capture its idyllic perfection. They will need assistance to understand how cold the temperature went when forbidden fruit was eaten and sin entered this tropical-like paradise. They will need to stand at the foot of the cross alongside strong able-bodied preachers to embrace the depth of what is being represented by a suffering Saviour. They will need to place their hand in the outstretched hand of another to grasp how the whole human family comes together for a funeral on Good Friday and for a family reunion on Easter Sunday morning. In re-creating this experience, listeners are invited to become eyewitnesses to a moment in time when the human race rises from the shadows of despair and cries out, "Christ is risen—he is risen indeed!" In this respect, it will be helpful for all who rise to the pulpit to remember the role they will play in facilitating this "lived experience" for the listener, which is ultimately enhanced by the "lived experience" of the preacher.

Thirdly, the hard claims of the gospel will only be heard by contemporary listeners as preachers give emphasis to the pastoral task. Effective preaching, whether in postmodern or post-Christian context, cannot happen outside of effective pastoral care and nurturing of one's Sunday morning audience. The importance of building relational bridges is critical if both preacher and congregant are going to be able to enter truly into each other's world. In this process, our first point of conversation will probably not be: "We implore you on Christ's behalf, be reconciled to God ... for now is the day of salvation" (2 Corinthians 5:20b, 6:2b). Rather the stronger approach is to begin with an invitation: "Come, taste and see that the Lord is good" (Psalm 34:8). Barbara Lundblad, in *Transforming the Stone–Preaching through Resistance to Change*, identifies the importance of calculated and well-thought-out evangelistic methodology as she unpacks insights from Mark's Gospel. Clearly, Jesus' first words in this instance were not "repent" but rather Jesus' inaugural message centred on the fact that the kingdom of God had come near (Mark 1:15). "Something new was breaking in.... Repentance becomes possible when God's grace comes near.... It is the assurance of grace that provides grounds for transformation."[20] Often preaching has failed to cultivate this soil in the past. History tells us that people will only risk moving toward radical social change when they perceive positive outcomes are possible. The starting point is always the good news that grace has moved into our neighbourhood and has decided to take up full residency in our midst.

A final insight evolving from Lundblad's perspective is that owning an aggressive homiletic in a postmodern/post-Christian context will require preachers to make specific calls to repentance and commitment. The challenge is to determine how best to do this.[21] As has been previously noted, people living in today's society have organized themselves in closed neighbourhoods. With privacy legislation, the guarding of our personal space and the limiting of online friends having become so much part of our cultural expression, the public bearing of spiritual beliefs and convictions is not always favourably received. Thus, in Salvation Army settings, we sometimes observe a hesitancy to step out to the mercy seat[22] or the altar. Many perceive it to be only a place for those who are in spiritual crises, rather than a place where the people of God can publicly proclaim "This is what I believe—and these are the convictions that are shaping my life." In this respect, the spirit of the Booths' homiletic is invited to live on through the faithfulness of Salvation Army preachers, who will not be overwhelmed by the tensions represented. One of the obvious strengths of the Booths' preaching method was that it invited people to make their faith public. As contemporary preachers negotiate their way through the myriad of contextual issues we have identified thus far, this element cannot be sacrificed. Preaching in The Salvation Army is still about proclaiming a disturbing gospel and calling people to a decision. It is still about giving listeners the opportunity to publicly announce and celebrate with the larger Body of Christ the convictions that are shaping their life of faith. Whether the call is for people to come and kneel or stand or to link hands with friends across the aisle or to come and be part of a tactile response,[23] the insistence is that there are tangible ways in which God's people would be invited to respond. In so doing, the philosophy of this homiletic affirms that faith is solidified in ways that are deeply significant when there is an outward demonstration of the inward workings of the Spirit. In seeking to honour the homiletical legacy of William and Catherine Booth, today's preachers should feel uninhibited in calling people to this place of public confirmation.

Fire Starter Three: Simplicity Lives On

The early preaching of The Salvation Army was based upon simplicity of approach and avoidance of churchliness. People today have a limited sense of church background and biblical story. They still require sermons that are presented in a language they can understand.

Commissioner Theodore Kitching, once a school teacher won to The Salvation Army from the Quakers and close confidant to both William and Bramwell Booth, pressed a significant agenda as it related to a simple approach to biblical proclamation:

> Do you speak so they understand? Not fine words or rolling rhetoric does the world need today—but the living truth in their plain mother tongue. The meaning of such

words as God, and the Devil, sin and righteousness, heaven
and hell, conscience and the great white throne is plain and
clear to all. Show people their sins—remind them of their
coffins—make them think of the judgment bar—tell them
of the cleansing blood—picture to them the bliss of being
saved and the agony of the lost.[24]

As has been previously identified, the need for simplicity of proclamation exists now more than ever before. In today's context,
people often come to the Christian story with limited to no frame of
reference. They have not attended Sunday school or Christian worship, and the songs that have been playing on their radios have not
included titles such as *Tell Me the Stories of Jesus–Write on My Heart
Every Word!* In view of this reality, Chris Altrock's *Preaching to Pluralists* argues the importance of today's preacher drawing listeners
into the Christian story by being highly attentive to language and
stories that are known to secular society. The key will be the utiliza-
tion of vocabulary, illustrations and images that will require no prior
knowledge of biblical story. Today's preachers are invited to see their
tutorial role in helping people become familiar with the basics of the
gospel and the biblical story, and to subsequently assist people in
processing the new theological ideas being presented. In this Altrock
argues further for the preacher to use language that will not only
convince the mind but also inflame the spirit.[25] Richard Lischer, in
The End of Words, advances this theme when he suggests how "the
hymnodist might have been speaking for the besieged preacher
when he asked, 'What language shall I borrow to thank thee dearest
friend?' "[26] The key insight toward which the preacher must now
navigate is the importance of not only capturing the attention of the
listener, but also knowing what to say and how to say it. Barbara
Brown Taylor, in *Speaking of Sin*, offers one of the most helpful treatments currently written on this tension. Arguing for the need of
today's preacher to address the themes of sin and damnation, repentance and salvation, Taylor recognizes these words will not be heard
easily.[27] Yet these kinds of words remain a necessary part of the

preacher's vocabulary, in order that the full impact of the gospel might be proclaimed:

> Abandoning the language of sin will not make sin go away. Human beings will continue to experience alienation, deformation, damnation and death no matter what we call them. Abandoning the language will simply leave us speechless before them, and increase our denial of their presence in our lives. Ironically, it will also weaken the language of grace, since the full impact of forgiveness cannot be felt apart from the full impact of what has been forgiven.[28]

In this respect, we understand how important it is that the themes of judgment and grace co-exist in preaching manuscripts. If we speak only of good news, how will we know the glory and the victory of that from which we have been saved? If we speak only of bad news, how will we know the hope that is ours in Jesus Christ? Good news is understood only as a positive message when we find the ability to place it alongside news that is not so positive. We could liken this reality to the setting of a group of seminary students in an introductory Greek course. Week after week through the semester, the professor has demanded long hours outside of class, learning extensive vocabulary and verb conjugations, working through endless New Testament translations. Suddenly, week 10 into the course, the professor announces, "No more homework this term! The remainder of course requirements will only take place in class." While this moment comes as relief and liberation for the student, it can only be understood and interpreted as such because of the point of contrast the student has known through the term. If endless homework and long study hours had not been part of the early learning experience, the opposite reality of *no homework* would not have the same effect. Similarly, only as listeners encounter the deep contrasts contained in the gospel message, i.e., the darkness of sin and the light of Christ's love, can there be a true interpretation of what it means to be redeemed by the grace of God.[29] Barbara Brown Taylor argues further that "sin becomes our only hope—the fire alarm that wakes us up to the possibility of true repentance."[30] The challenge becomes the manner in which preachers will now engage their talking about sin. Thomas Long, recently quoted in *Does Anyone Believe in Sin Anymore?*, speaks further into this issue by identifying the manner through which preaching about sin is heard:

> If your church is teaching that working on the Sabbath is sinful, or that drinking or abortions or gossip is sinful, it's likely that your leaders don't understand you.... Preachers need to be careful when talking about sin; using the word pretty well guarantees that some people will mishear what the word means. Some will hear it as a shame-filled word, or a word that applies to bad activities, or as something that psycho-therapy helps you get away from—the preacher needs to creatively and imaginatively teach the biblical understanding of God.[31]

While much could be suggested as to what is necessary for creative and imaginative rendering of biblical truths, Barbara Brown Taylor presses preachers to think about "the sparks that must jump between the words of the preacher and the realities they describe."[32]

> I do not believe there is any adequate substitute for this language. But in order to keep it alive, each of us must do our own work—not only the work of diving deep into human experience to the find the realities the words describe, but also the work of bringing these words to life by clothing them in our flesh. There is no reason why anyone should ever believe our talk of God's transforming power unless they see that transformation taking place in us, in the world. We are the people God has chosen to embody the gospel. Our lives are God's sign language in a sin-sick world. And God has promised us the grace we need to point the way home.[33]

Again we can imagine on heaven's balcony yet another boisterous "amen" is coming from the mouths of William and Catherine Booth. This is the message of the early Salvation Army that believed in the importance of proclaiming a gospel that could be understood and embraced by all. If Taylor's argument holds ground, it is evident that the spoken word of the preacher, now perhaps more than ever, must be linked with the embodied word of the preacher. In this way, the language of salvation will not be sacrificed, but rather put side by side with real, holy people, thus waking up contemporary listeners to the new life that can be found in Christ and Christ alone.

Fire Starter Four: The Power of Personal Testimony

The early preachers of The Salvation Army believed in the power of personal testimony (or story) to authenticate the gospel message to the unbeliever. Postmodern/post-Christian listeners will be convinced more than anything by the power of personal story rather than lengthy theological discourses.

As has been previously stated, "the chief arsenal of the Salvationist preacher is experience. Never does one tire in proclaiming, 'I know in whom I have believed' " (2 Timothy 1:12).[34] William and Catherine Booth recognized the importance of this preaching strategy and made their early converts their leading evangelists. As drunkards and derelicts told their stories of extreme transformation, they could not help but arrest the attention of those who had known them in their former state. The retelling of personal faith stories authenticated the truth of gospel claims to Victorian listeners. Such is the great need of today, as preachers attempt to convince skeptical listeners of the truth within the gospel's difficult claims. Herein one encounters yet another vibrant example of how the Booth homiletic can have relevance to contemporary preaching. This is reinforced by conversation already circulating in the homiletical community. Chris Altrock, in *Preaching to Pluralists*, points to the manner in which "the Bible tells me so" or "this objective evidence tells me so" simply will not sell. But rather, congregations will be most persuaded of the truth of a claim when it is confirmed in the story of a person. Evangelism works best today when it demonstrates the plausibility and authenticity of the gospel through an individual's lived experience and the boldness to claim, "This is my story, this is my song!"[35]

In a cultural context where authoritarian type leadership is now being redefined, what Altrock offers makes good sense. Postmodern/post-Christian thinkers will not respond to truth forced upon them, because they are essentially convinced that there are many valid versions of truth to be embraced. What works for one may not work for another, but (according to them) it is all truth. Advancing the need for the preacher to continue speaking through personal story therefore becomes essential, for it becomes the means through which one truth claim will stand out over another. Don Posterski, quoted in *Church Next*, further argues how the world needs to see what the Christian life looks like. "People who think God is unnecessary, or just optional in life, need fresh images of how life is meant to be. They need hard evidence that following Jesus really makes a difference." It is only as the gospel is held up in this way, that people will have the ability to see the feasible alternatives Scripture provides.[36] Holding to the priority of this emphasis, not only in evangelistic strategies, but also in preaching, becomes essential. The gospel is no longer simply a truth to be defended but rather now a testimony to be proclaimed. In authenticating the power of an experiential faith, through spoken personal story, contemporary listeners are given greater reason to embrace the difficult claims of the gospel, even if it seems a message initially harsh and hard to hear. The primary argument remains that truth will have more possibility of singing into someone's ear, if it is first played in a key with which they can resonate. Herein, the value of preaching that speaks into the heartbeat of human experience and gives witness to a true and relevant salvation cannot be missed for what it brings to the renewing of society.

Robinson and Wall, in *Called to Be Church*, demonstrate how this was particularly true in the Apostle Peter's life. Peter was a preacher who knew of what and whom he spoke. Peter was one who had known both failure and forgiveness. He had encountered the "God of second chances." The man who preached God's grace and forgiveness had experienced the same for himself.[37] Emerging from this, Peter demonstrates how it is possible to preach a daring and provocative sermon as exemplified in Acts 2:38: "Repent and be baptized every one of you, in the name of Jesus Christ for the forgiveness of your sins. And you will receive the gift of the Holy Spirit." The arrogance of this message is tempered through the voice of a preacher who has known his own need for the mercy and forgiveness he proclaims.

Fire Starter Five: A Continuing Burden for Suffering Humanity

The early preaching of The Salvation Army was based upon a deep burden for suffering humanity. Similarly, people living in a postmodern/post-Christian context are seeking a new sense of community. They will respond favourably to those who communicate a message that they matter to others.

In recognizing this contextual dynamic, sociologist Leonard Sweet presses to the heart of the matter when he observes the way in which people are finding their communal connecting points in society. He asks quite pointedly why Times Square is the most popular place to greet the new millennium. Why are coffee bars the new dating place? Why is the Internet becoming less an information medium than a social medium, with more and more people logging on, not to gain information, but to hear "You've got mail" and even to find love online.[38]

While the sense of community described by Sweet is notably different from the context of Victorian England, it is evident that there is a continuing quest of individuals to find a place in community. Victorians found connecting points leaning out their windows, talking to their neighbours across the lane or sitting on their steps or playing in the streets. The point is that there was connection. In a postmodern/post-Christian setting connection now takes place at the local coffee shop, in online chat rooms, through Facebook or Twitter or through cellular texting. The need for human beings to connect to each other has not fallen off the radar screen, but it is a need that has been reshaped and redefined. What remains is the primary longing of human beings to matter to someone else. This becomes essential to the overall well-being of both the individual and society at large. This is where the Booth homiletic again becomes relevant to the preaching of the disturbing claims of the gospel. In the life and witness of William and Catherine Booth, people mattered. The well-being and spiritual state of those to whom they preached was their number one priority. All of their lives were given to save the poor people to whom no one else seemed to be bothering to throw a lifeline.

How then will the disturbing claims of the gospel be heard by today's contemporary listener? They will be heard as individuals genuinely sense the preacher's care and concern for others. This is confirmed by Aristotle's communication theory,[39] which stresses the importance of ethos to persuade listeners to believe a message spoken to them. The issue then becomes the preacher's "withness" toward people. Leonora Tubbs Tisdale, in *Preaching as Local Theology and Folk Art*, reinforces this theme when she suggests much of preaching today suffers from an " 'over-againstness' in which the preacher mounts to the pulpit to cajole, correct, challenge, instruct or in some manner 'shape up' the congregation. The challenge of the 21st-century pulpit is for pastors to reclaim a renewed 'withness' moving to the pulpit out of the midst of the congregation, giving witness to the struggles and questions that emerge from the experiences of everyday life. When people sense you are 'with' them, and they see the commonality of the human road travelled, they will be far more willing to stand before a God who confronts and challenges us all."[40]

To this end, today's preacher will be required, as he or she ascends to the pulpit Sunday after Sunday, to determine what kind of people are sitting before them in the pew. Through what kind of lens are they viewing congregants? As Craig Loscalzo, in *Apologetic Preaching*, asks, "Do they see a sinner damned and condemned or do they see a person created in the image and likeness of God, for whom Christ died and with whom God longs to have a loving and lasting relationship?"[41] Herein, we encounter again the heartbeat of William Booth: "O the poor, poor, people—to save these people"[42] and the longing that all those within the Founder's sphere of influence would come to reach their fullest potential in Christ. On this note, the Booth homiletic proclaims again its relevance to address the complex issues of contemporary preaching. Hard messages will always stand a greater chance of being heard when the receiver senses the genuine care and compassion of the sender. Preachers are encouraged to develop strong pastoral relationships with their congregants in order to achieve this goal.[43]

Fire Starter Six: The Centrality of Scripture to Preaching

The early preaching of The Salvation Army was enlivened by the centrality of Scripture to the preaching task. Contemporary preaching will only experience renewal as preachers centre themselves again toward this same authority.

Echoing words that have already reverberated through these pages, the conviction of William Booth was that the Bible was "a fire escape by which men could be pulled out of the raging fire of sin; a lifeboat by which they could be rescued from the stormy waves ... a ladder up which they could climb to the golden gates of the City of God."[44] Within this statement the performative power of Scripture is isolated as that which brings hope and salvation into a person's life. Upon this rock we stand—all other ground is sinking sand! Something was clearly alive in the early homiletic of The Salvation Army. The proclaimed Word actually did something; it saved; it rescued; it lifted broken people up to the golden gates of heaven. Upon the authority of this sacred Word was this saving work accomplished.

Similarly, the call to contemporary preachers is to make sure something living is represented in our pulpits. This expression of life is brought about by the authority of God-breathed, God-inspired Scripture that has gripped the heart and mind of the preacher and infused energy and new life first and foremost into him or her. Thomas Long warns how "too many preachers have become disengaged from Scripture. Unless they are alive in Scripture, they will never be alive to listeners."[45] Michael Quicke, in *360 Degree Preaching*, builds on this emphasis by stressing the importance of the preacher's personal engagement to the biblical text. Quicke says: "First open Scripture and experience God's Word for yourself. If it does not come alive to the preachers' heads and hearts, to their eyes, ears and senses, it is unlikely to come alive to listeners."[46]

As the preacher steps into this process, a word of warning is merited: "Don't be afraid if this authoritative, living, breathing, active Word unsettles you! Don't falter if this Word causes you to struggle; or causes you to stop in your own tracks and re-evaluate the direction of your life. Don't be dissuaded when this Word takes you to task and demands changes in attitude and action!" Recognizing the enormous challenge this is for the preacher, Dietrich Bonhoeffer, in *Meditating on the Word*, presses the preacher to acknowledge the fear that can often hold us at a distance to the true power of the living Word:

> But we are not only afraid of ourselves and of self-discovery, we are much more afraid of God—that he may disturb us and discover who we really are, that he may take us with him into his solitude and deal with us according to his will. We are afraid of such lonely, awful encounters with God, and we avoid them, so that he may not suddenly come too near to us.[47]

With this said, perhaps it is at this juncture that the key is discovered as to how today's preacher can truly open the door and proclaim a disturbing gospel. It only happens as God comes near to the preacher and we truly allow this experience to unsettle us, in order that we might unsettle others. Only as preachers open themselves to the authoritative power of the Word will something spark life and energy into cold and empty places. This was the driving conviction of the early evangelists of The Salvation Army that now challenges the contemporary preacher to action.

Acknowledging the Difficulties of Reviving the Fires

While I have advocated for an assimilation of a Booth homiletic as a means of challenging the status quo of a settled society, we give consideration now to elements of this preaching approach that will require reshaping to be truly effective in a postmodern/post-Christian context. For the purpose of this final summary, we will explore two distinct areas: 1) the tone of a re-contextualized Booth homiletic[48] and 2) the ultimate destination of a *new Salvationist homiletic*. The goal is not to discredit the value the Booths' approach to preaching brings to postmodern pulpits, but to point to those areas in which a further reshaping and redefining can assist in strengthening the ties contemporary preaching might have to that of the Victorian era.

If today's preachers are going to be successful in causing the postmodern/post-Christian generation to "stop, look and listen" to the gospel, it is essential that the tone of the early Booth homiletic be evaluated as it is placed alongside the possibility of a new Salvationist homiletic. Since we no longer live in a context where authority is a given for the preacher to speak as the ultimate voice of truth, some rethinking is necessary in this area. Postmodern/post-Christian listeners will not be persuaded by those who project an aura of harsh judgment, nor will they be impressed by preachers who seem to set themselves apart as better than others. While this is not to suggest that this was the intention of the Booths in their preaching approach, what is recognized is the possibility of it being heard in this manner within a contemporary context. One cannot simply excavate phrases from the Booths' sermons and assume this language will be received in the same manner it was in Victorian England. Rather, it must be acknowledged that the aggressive tone of their preaching risks the possibility of alienating listeners, instead of drawing them closer. What is needed, therefore, is not an energy that is determined to shake slumbering sinners awake but rather an energy that is now aggressively inviting listeners into a profound life-changing event, as revealed through God's Word. The aggressive tone of the preacher is to be generated, not so much by an urgency to straighten people up, as by an earnest invitation for people to come and see for themselves what God has done in the past and is doing in the world today. The face-to-face showdown that has previously defined confrontational preaching is reshaped and strengthened by an urgency to invite people into a depth of new experience. This form of homiletic is ultimately not about hostile engagement but about an energetic, passionate invitation to come and taste of the goodness of the Lord. Thomas Long best captures the intention of this argument in his cave analogy:

> Imagine that the biblical text for next Sunday's sermon is not a piece of literature but a deep and mysterious cave. The preacher is the trained explorer of caves who descends into this one, flashlight and ropes in hand, filled with excitement of discovery. Others have explored this cave before, indeed the preacher has read their accounts, studied their maps, been excited by the sights they have seen, marvelled at the treasures they have discovered, and is impelled by their assurances that there are new treasures yet to be found. The preacher moves even deeper into the cave.... He wanders through alluring grottos, only to find they end in cold, blank walls. He shines his light across chasms too wide for him to cross with the equipment that he has. He inches his way down a high and narrow ledge, almost losing his footing and tumbling into the black infinity below. Suddenly, he turns a corner and there it is, what he has been looking for all along. Perhaps it is a waterfall tumbling from a great height to the floor below. Or perhaps it is an enormous stalactite, an icicle eons old which overwhelms him by its sheer size. Or maybe his flashlight has illumined a wall of gems, filling the dark space with dancing fire and color. He stands before the sight in a moment of awe and silence. Then, knowing what he must do, he carefully retraces his path, scrambles to the mouth of the cave, and with the dirt of the journey still on his face and his flashlight waving excitedly, he calls to those who have been waiting on him, "Come on, have I got something to show you!"[49]

One has to take note that when Long's explorer finally exits the cave, his first words are not: "Pay attention here folks! You are all in such big trouble! You won't believe what I've just seen! You are really in for it now!" Rather, the aggression and earnestness of a new Salvationist homiletic is inspired by a mandate to get the listener down into the cave; to see truth first hand; to take in the overwhelming sights of tumbling waterfalls and glistening gems and gigantic icicles. "Come with me," says today's Salvationist preacher. "Let me show you what I have seen!" In this respect, confrontational preaching assumes a different tone, and adopts a different approach. The intention is not to tell people what their problem is, but to let them see it for themselves as they unpack first-hand the implications of what they see. In many respects, it is a recasting of Isaiah 6:1-5 in which the prophet Isaiah enters into the most holy place of God. He sees the Lord high and exalted on his throne and the train of his robe fills the temple. As Isaiah finds his way into his own homiletical cave, he is brought face-to-face with this magnificent vision of who God is. There is no preacher present in this moment announcing Isaiah's sin and unworthiness to be in God's presence. Isaiah sees it for himself. "Woe to me! I cried. I am ruined! For I am a man of unclean lips, and I live among a people of unclean lips, and my eyes have seen the King, the Lord Almighty" (Isaiah 6:5). The goal of aggressive confrontational preaching in a postmodern/post-Christian context is to bring people face-to-face with a vision of who God is, and to allow them to see for themselves who they are in response. Adjusting the tone of the message to reflect the wonder and joy and adventure of this journey will be critical to realizing this outcome. As listeners are brought into a depth of textual experience, they will more readily allow us to dialogue with them about the essential issues of faith. The primary point remains that today's listeners must be convinced that there is something worth seeing. A new Salvationist homiletic (which seeks to recapture the essence of the Booth homiletic) must therefore, re-create through its tone and energy, a vision of the ultimate glory and hope of the kingdom of God.

Preachers who seek to re-contextualize a Booth homiletic into a new Salvationist homiletic will need to be sensitive as to how an audience is defined within this approach to preaching. In the Victorian England context, the Booths saw their primary congregation as the working-class poor. They saw the impoverished and marginalized as those who were sitting on the fringes of religion. Recognizing the social gap that existed, the Booths determined where their message would go. With this said, it could be argued that early Salvationists resolved to preach into the gap. Significant change was taking place in society as the effects of the Industrial Revolution emerged. Cultural norms were being reorganized as people were finding their way from rural settings into the cities. Today's preacher must now stand at the intersection of Culture Street and Faith Boulevard and recognize the different way the socio-religious gap of our day is presented. Those who sit on the fringe of the Christian faith are no longer just the working-class poor. While the ministry of The Salvation Army will continue to recognize this audience as their primary target group, preachers of all persuasions must see how much wider the harvest field has become and how much more complex are the roadblocks before them.

Victorian preachers could assume when they stood in the pulpit to preach that those within their hearing had some sense of affinity and connection to the truth presented. This, however, is no longer the case in our current culture. Contemporary preachers can expect much greater difficulty in achieving congregational engagement and response. Consequently, the scope and destination of a new Salvationist homiletic becomes redefined as preachers recognize how significantly their audiences have changed. Now more than ever, it is a global audience that is coming from all walks of life, bringing with it a diversity of faith perspectives and all the baggage of postmodern/post-Christian thinking. Most striking of all roadblocks is the assertion people readily make that suggests they are "OK!" They have no need for the truth of God. The challenge for today's preacher is to present the possibility of an alternative perspective and an alternative reality. Our goal is to reach those settled in the "way things are." The key will be to invite people to ask new questions about their current state of existence and where this is actually taking them. The goal is not manipulation but to facilitate a movement in perspective that will invite listeners to see how a God-centred life not only improves the present, but also ensures a future filled with the certainty of all God is and all his Word has promised.

Conclusion

Through the contents of this chapter, readers have been invited to dream new possibilities as to what biblical preaching could look like in a postmodern/post-Christian era. Arguing for the assimilation of a Booth homiletic into what we have labelled as a new Salvationist homiletic, the premise of this discussion has been grounded on the paralleling of historical and cultural claims. These now seem to connect effectively with each other.

Firstly, the homiletic of the early Salvation Army saw its primary goal as offering new realities for broken people. Today, people want life played in a new key. They have grown tired of the same repeating melody that lands them in the same predictable place of despair, day in and day out. While there is a desire to "sing a new song" as the psalmist would say (Psalm 144:9), people struggle to find their way through the dissonance and dissatisfaction of life. Both historical and contemporary expressions of preaching recognize the urgency of the work that is to be done. Broken people need hope. Sin is still our greatest problem and acknowledging this is our greatest means toward realizing an experience of new life, found in God alone.

Secondly, to advance this agenda the Booth homiletic is now re-contextualized to become a new Salvationist homiletic. In so doing, emphasis is given to help the congregant see the great contrast that exists between the darkness of God's wrath versus the light of divine love. This will be most effectively conveyed by simplicity of homiletical approach, to which postmodern/post-Christian thinkers say, "This is exactly what we need, because we do not always know and understand the language that you speak!" Authenticating this with the power of personal story, listeners will applaud this homiletical effort as one that is clearly recognizing the manner in which contemporary culture best processes new ideas and images.

Thirdly, as today's preachers embrace the legacy of the Booth homiletic, they will emphasize the centrality of Scripture in the preaching task. Listeners and preachers alike are invited to see the Word of God as that which is alive and active, a vibrant holy word that has the power to improve the future as it disturbs the present!

Fourthly, recognizing the need to be fully abreast of the challenges this preaching paradigm will bring, contemporary preachers acknowledge that the tone of a re-contextualized Booth homiletic will need to be reshaped. Hostile, harsh confrontation between the pulpit and the pew will do little to woo and persuade today's post-modern/post-Christian seeker. Rather, today's confrontational homiletic must be understood as an invitational homiletic that seeks to call people energetically and passionately to sacred spaces where they can meet God face-to-face and see the reality of their spiritual condition for themselves. Only from this place can the deeper conversations of faith evolve. In the end, it will be about a confrontation—but it will be orchestrated in such a way as to make sojourners ready and open for both the weightiness and wonder of what they experience.

Finally, those who adopt a new Salvationist homiletic are urged to reassess the destination of their preaching. Today's audience no longer lives at the same cultural and spiritual address as those who were part of Victorian times. Knowing who presently sits on the fringes of faith is critical in deciding to whom the saving words of a disturbing gospel should now be delivered.

CHAPTER 6

RETURNING TO OUR PLACE OF BEGINNING

"There is no improving the future, without disturbing the present and the difficulty is to get people to be willing to be disturbed!"
—Catherine Booth, 1880

A S HISTORY AND HOMILETIC HAVE MET IN THE ARENA OF these pages, we pause to bring this part of our conversation to a conclusion. The primary concern is to ensure that questions raised thus far have received adequate discussion and sufficient resolve where possible. If some ambiguity still exists, let this chapter be a means of acknowledging the same and offering some further assessment of preaching conversations that may follow.

Returning to our place of beginning, the homiletic of William and Catherine Booth entered onto centre stage of Victorian England in 1865 with drums beating and horns blaring. It was an impressive entrance, not only because of the energy and vitality it represented, but also because of the significant results it was seeing in terms of lives influenced for the gospel's sake. Catherine Booth was convinced of the importance of preaching a disturbing gospel. The intent was to unsettle people who had become complacent to religious experience and to cause them to take notice of the truths of God. History has given testimony to the effectiveness of this emphasis. As a result, we have entertained the question as to whether this historical homiletic has any relevance to the postmodern/ post-Christian context in which we serve. If only for the reason of the historical results noted, we initially hope that a connection is possible and that this might spark new fires in our pulpits today.

Diving into both the complexities of the Victorian era in which the Booths ministered and the realities of our postmodern/ post-Christian context, we have been led to see both the commonalities and differences of these time periods. Postmodern/ post-Christian sojourners live at a very different address to their Victorian counterparts, yet there are some cultural and spiritual realities that we share in common. Bringing these two worlds together, we begin to see ways in which the confrontational approach of the Booth homiletic might be re-contextualized to address 21st-century preaching challenges. Entering into the pulpit of today's preacher is a new Salvationist homiletic that pleads its relevance for this present age. Particular characteristics define the shape and design of this new emerging homiletic. It is also a preaching approach that seeks to respond to specific questions.

Firstly, this new Salvationist homiletic calls preachers to remember their first purposes. We preach Jesus Christ crucified and risen from the dead! We preach the hope emanating from the empty tomb! We preach "God so loved the world that he gave his one and only son, that whoever believes in him shall not perish but have eternal life" (John 3:16). We preach something of eternal importance. In the murkiness of societal complacency, we have been given a message that has the power to shatter the darkness of the age in which we live. As cultural agendas press their weight upon us to assimilate within their norms, today's preacher says, "Hold on—we've got something different to offer the world and we believe this message can lead us to a better future, as it improves the place where we stand today."

Secondly, this new Salvationist homiletic seeks to address how it is possible for those who lack affinity and relationship to the Church, to truly embrace biblical and spiritual claims.[1] Realistically speaking, we ask how listeners will be persuaded toward these truths. Grounding the marriage between the Booth homiletic and a new Salvationist homiletic is a firm belief that the difficult claims of the gospel should not be sacrificed on the altar of cultural discomfort. It is in the contrasting of judgment and grace that people today are truly able to see the power of the experience into which they are invited. By energetic, creative recreating of biblical texts, the preacher will enable listeners to see where their stories connect with God's story.

Thirdly, in negotiating our way further through this homiletical conversation, we see that this new Salvationist homiletic seeks to address how the preacher regains credibility as one who has a necessary and valuable message to bring to those both inside and outside the experience of faith.[2] In this respect, the vitality of what the preacher represents, both from a textual and personal perspective, contributes to that which will stimulate the heart and mind of the listener. Today's preachers who seek to embrace the new Salvationist homiletic will have to be sensitive to the fact that the audience before them is skeptical and lacks trust. Postmodern/post-Christian thinkers will not be manipulated into faith. Rather, the preacher whom they believe to be genuine and authentic in the representation of truth will be successful in gaining their attention and hearing. The value of strong pastoral connections linked with the uncompromised integrity of the preacher will do much to solidify this relationship.

Fourthly, we must ask the question whether a re-contextualized Booth homiletic is only relevant to the kind of audience it first addressed, i.e. the working-class poor.[3] In this respect, assimilation of this preaching approach invites today's sermon writers to redefine where socio-religious gaps are now evident. It is where the gospel is not reaching—where good news is not being proclaimed, where people are not intersecting with the truths of Scripture—that this form of preaching must go. Utilizing the strategic principles of the Booths, which argued for passionate proclamation, simplicity, creativity and grounding in the centrality of Scripture alone, will do much to capture the attention of complacent listeners.

Fifthly, given the cultural landscape of the day, the question looms as to whether it is confrontational preaching that is needed or whether this approach is too intrusive for those who have placed themselves within closed neighbourhoods.[4] Before the final word is spoken and the doors are closed on this discussion, let it be clearly stated: confrontational preaching in a postmodern/post-Christian context should no longer be about hostile face-to-face engagement.

Rather, it is about an invitational homiletic that facilitates a way for listeners to get face-to-face with God and inside the truth of his Word. Herein, preachers are challenged to find new ways to communicate the sheer wonder of what they experienced as they prepared for the preaching event. In this respect, we are reminded, by nature of the pulpit-to-pew relationship, that the preacher will always have the advantage of being the first on-site investigative reporter to the text's unfolding drama. Ours is the privilege to invite listeners inside the text to taste and see for themselves all the Word has to reveal. Future homiletical forums that focus preachers toward finding more effective ways to unpack the experience of a biblical text will do much to cultivate fresh air and new energy in today's pulpit. What is known for sure is that the wonder of this experience cannot be communicated to others if preachers have not found the wonder of the text for themselves. When this happens, our own lives are jarred to see the new realities God has placed within our reach. My prayer is that God would help preachers to be disturbed so they can disturb others.

Finally, as the voice of current Salvation Army preachers weighed into this debate, the absence of *disturbing gospel language* was noted. No mention was made of terms such as heaven or hell, eternal judgment or guilt as it relates to personal sin.[5] Ultimately then, what is gained with the inclusion of these themes in preaching? What is lost when this language is not present? It becomes evident as this debate draws to a close that what is lost is what is truly at stake for the post-modern/post-Christian listener. Holding the absolute certainty of eternal judgment as a marker and recognizing the accounting each person will have to do one day before the throne of God, preaching becomes a huge disconnect if somewhere listeners are not being called to think toward these themes. Does this mean the gospel becomes one which only engenders fear, and conversion is the result of a desire not to be left behind or shut out in the cold where entrance into the kingdom will never be possible? The point remains that this is a portion of the God story (as demonstrated in the sermon sample provided in PART II). One cannot ignore this truth simply because it is weighted and uncomfortable. Nor can detours be taken around the prescriptive claims of Scripture which call for holy living and sinless perfection in a believer's life ("But just as he who called you is holy, so be holy in all that you do, for it is written: 'Be holy, because I am holy' " (1 Peter 1:15-16)). In this respect we are left holding both the burden and the privilege of the preaching task. To challenge the condition of the human soul outside of the experience of salvation is the weighted responsibility of every preacher; but to hold out the lifeline through which new life and hope is realized remains the greatest joy and privilege of ministry. This is especially true when we see evidence of response and receptivity to the transforming Word we proclaim.

In conclusion, no matter what cultural context we might find ourselves in, this journey from the early pulpit of The Salvation Army to our current day reminds us that all preachers are called to proclaim the fullness of God's Word. This is how we point to what life and relationship with God are truly all about. Does this mean every sermon will lend itself to these themes of hell and eternal judgment? Probably not! But today's preachers must, at some point, make a full diagnosis of the reality that sits before them. As the fullness of God's story is told, preachers will be forced to acknowledge that all of humanity is terminally ill with a disease called sin. Unless people are caused to see the hopelessness of their current condition and the hope-filled remedy Christ has provided, they will never be free from the bondage that they know now. They will never be well.

Where does this ultimately bring those who would dare to preach God's Word in the arena of those who are consumed and overwhelmed by the realities of postmodern/post-Christian living? Perhaps it is a return to the words of William Booth that helps us the most. His encouragement was to "preach as one dying man to another."[6] If we were to imagine that within the next hour all who were in our congregation were to be ushered to heaven's door, would this change our message? If anything, the great parting word from this intersecting of history and homiletic is to acknowledge the tremendous privilege and responsibility that can be owned by today's preacher to say something to listeners that truly matters! To preach as if something is at stake; to risk that the message may not be a popular one, but it is the one that God requires in this time and space. Therefore, preachers are called to utilize all the tools and strategies of homiletical thought to find new creative and engaging ways to talk about the sin problem of our world.

As cultural tensions continue to create detours and road blocks, the hope is that history and homiletic will bring us to meaningful crossroads where we will realize we need not be held hostage to the trends of the day.[7] Rather, the vision and the hope is that preachers would rise up with strong and vibrant voices that are not afraid to upset the status quo of society—for post-Booth preachers to see new possibilities for a struggling world; to see how society can be changed by both experience and first-hand knowledge of God's eternal truth and promises contained within a disturbing gospel. The stakes in this are high, " ... we have this treasure in jars of clay to show that this all surpassing power is from God and not from us" (2 Corinthians 4:7). With the confidence of this promise, we go forth to unsettle and disturb. We go forth to say something to a broken world that truly will make a difference!

PART II

RESOURCES FOR THE PREACHER

CHAPTER 7

HOW TO PREACH A
DISTURBING GOSPEL

Moving Listeners Beyond Kansas

I N ONE MOMENT, DOROTHY IS A SIMPLE FARM GIRL LIVING IN
Kansas with her aunt and three hired hands. She is convinced,
"There is no place like home," and the certainty of this sentiment finds its definition through the close connection of
family, the familiar landscape of the surrounding fields and the
faithful following of a beloved dog named Toto. Then suddenly the
familiar is disturbed. We know the story well. A raging tornado
approaches and uproots everything in its path. While the rest of the
family takes shelter in a locked storm cellar, young Dorothy dashes
to safety inside the farmhouse. Subsequently the force of the wind
blows out a window frame and knocks Dorothy unconscious. With
the stage now set for the 1939 American musical film, *The Wizard of
Oz*, Dorothy awakens to her new reality. To her shock and surprise,
she discovers her farmhouse carried far away from that which is
familiar. As she steps into a land steeped in the fantasy of witches
and wizards, munchkins and talking scarecrows, it does not take
Dorothy long to figure out, "I'm not in Kansas anymore."

This well-known film is an effective example of what dislocation
looks like. In one defined moment, everything is comfortable and
familiar. Then suddenly, we find ourselves navigating a new course

with no previously established GPS points of co-ordinate. Life as we know it has been disturbed. While tornados will not necessarily be our cause of disruption, the point is that some applied force "unsettles" the routine predictability of the "settled." Preaching that is to arrest the attention of today's postmodern/post-Christian listener must search for pressure points or confronting influences that will achieve this same unsettling effect. The goal is to cause those caught up in the frantic pace of life to come to a halt and dislocate from the familiar. It will involve a turning of direction; a tuning into a new station; an adjusting to a new divine frequency that will dislocate listeners from the "familiar sights of Kansas," toward that which is life-changing and new.

With this purpose in mind, when Jesus preached, he often spoke in parables. The goal was to shake up previously formed perspectives with the intent of first getting listeners' attention and then, secondly, to open up new windows of understanding. We can only imagine the gasps in the crowd when Jesus spoke about a boss who paid one-hour workers the same salary as those who had put in a full 12-hour shift (see Matthew 20:1-16). Surely, there were those who questioned the sensibility of a shepherd who would leave 99 sheep unprotected out on the hillside, while he went off foolishly searching for the one that had run away (see Luke 15:1-7). What kind of livelihood would he have left, if wild animals had attacked the majority of this flock while he was on his private search-and-rescue mission? Consider as well what the reaction would have been to a story about a farmer who goes out to sow his seed, absolutely indifferent to the lack of favourable soil conditions upon which some of the seed falls (see Luke 8:1-15). Someone in the crowd had to be asking, "Is this person out of his mind? Smart farmers calculate how they can achieve their greatest yield. What is the sense in throwing seed in places you know will not achieve a return?"

While we could cite many other parabolic examples, we observe within each of these instances how the normal, the routine and the predictable are upset. Listeners are compelled, naturally, to lean forward to figure out what is going on. Note here, textual tensions do not distract people from the text, but rather serve to draw them closer. Listeners want to figure out the mystery that is before them.

Using parabolic structure as a foundation for developing strategies to preach a disturbing gospel, we draw insight from French philosopher Paul Ricoeur (1913-2005). He contributes significantly to biblical interpretation by identifying the general pattern of a parable: firstly to *orientate* the listener to a new context, secondly to *disorientate* the listener through exposure to textual tensions, and then to finally *re-orientate* with the intent of theologically gluing back together that which has been fragmented and disturbed.[1] Ricoeur argued how this particular model was instrumental in startling New Testament audiences toward the truths Jesus proclaimed:

> The parables as stories take the reader to the point where the course of ordinary life is broken, an intensification of the everyday emerges. The unexpected happens; a strange world of meaning is projected which challenges, jars, disorients our everyday vision precisely by both showing us the limits to the everyday and projecting the limit of the character of the whole.[2]

As we place these insights alongside that which defines a Booth homiletic, we recognize the resource the parabolic model provides for assimilating past and present preaching approaches. Ricoeur assists us in seeing this possibility by emphasizing how the language of the parables is paradoxical and exaggerated (hyperbolic), while at the same time realistic. It is an instance of "extravagance which interrupts the superbly peaceful course of action and which constitutes the extraordinary within the ordinary."[3] Drawing together the picture that is emerging, we realize how succinctly the purpose of the parable parallels that which we are trying to accomplish in the application of a new Salvationist homiletic. Our goal is to "interrupt the superbly peaceful course of things," to "jar and disorientate" in order that the imagination and the human will might be opened to new possibilities. The benefit of Ricoeur's approach to interpreting the parables is that it provides a framework for the preaching of all kinds of biblical texts. More specifically, it provides a structure through which today's preacher can approach difficult and sensitive texts that will call the listener to leave behind the comforts of Kansas.

Preaching to Orientate/Disorientate/Re-orientate

Strategy #1—Textual Orientation

Using as a sample text Matthew 25:1-13, the Parable of the Wise and Foolish Bridesmaids, we move to unpack how a sermon is shaped, if Ricoeur's orientate/disorientate/re-orientate model provides the structure upon which preaching ideas are hung.

Firstly, the preacher must identify what is generally going on in the story. What is the setting? Who are the characters? What action is taking place? What challenges are immediately obvious? Upon what general history and context is the text building? For example, is this in sequence with other stories Jesus is telling? Is it part of a larger narrative? Where does the parable fit in terms of the overall chronology of Jesus' life and ministry? Note that the goal in this first section of the sermon is to lead the listener systematically toward the strangeness of the biblical narrative. This section will require detailed thought and preparation, with special attention to the background details that define the context in which the story was first heard. Simplicity of approach will be most important. This is not the place in the sermon to unpack complex theological ideas or to offer detailed word studies. Rather the goal is to launch the text and get the basic elements of the story airborne for preaching. Simply put, orientation works to align the listener to the basic gist of the story.

Secondly, in order to get the text launched for listeners, preachers must intentionally work to recreate an experience of the text. Note here a clear distinction we are making. Explanation is not our goal. Rather we are aiming toward a vibrant active experience of the text in which listeners might be caught up in the action that is unfolding. Preachers achieve this goal only as they aim to experience the text first-hand for themselves. Diligent and thorough exegesis will be essential. While limited time constraints may tempt the preacher to take the fast drive-by tour, preachers who are serious about communicating a compelling word will take the time to get off the bus and explore what is not so obvious from the text's roadside view.

This will require interaction with the biblical characters and a willingness to sit in different vantage points of the story. Specific questions will assist in unpacking the depth of what lies buried in the text. For example:

1. What is it like to be one of the wise bridesmaids?
2. What conversation might we hear sitting alongside them?
3. What is the perceived attitude of the wise bridesmaids toward the foolish bridesmaids?
4. What emotions are present as lamps begin to flicker toward the midnight hour?
5. What advances the role of the foolish bridesmaids in the story?
6. How does the telling of the parable keep the tension alive?
7. What initial impact does the story have upon the preacher?
8. Whose side do we find ourselves leaning toward? To whom are we favourably disposed?
9. Who has the power?
10. What will be required for tensions to be resolved?
11. Where do we see our own reflection mirrored in the text?

To achieve effective engagement with the biblical text, preachers will need to do more than just knock on the text's front door. It will require a deliberate moving in where the true tensions of the text can be experienced first-hand.

Thirdly, to achieve an effective orientation to the biblical story, preachers are encouraged to look for contemporary images to enliven the text to a modern-day perspective. For instance, if in our modern-day context, we run out of batteries at the midnight hour, what are our options to solve our problem? Chances are we are going to go out and look for an all-night convenience store. When the guest of honour finally arrives, how would we respond, if suddenly the story took on a 21st-century look? Think about how technology would respond and how we would instantly try to get the word out that the bridegroom had finally arrived. Surely there was at least one bridesmaid who felt a compelling urge to update her Facebook status. We can only imagine the hum in cyberspace as social media buzzed with the news that was finally breaking. While due care will be taken to not allow contemporary images to overtake the text, effective engagement will be achieved when the listener discovers how his or her own world finds parallel alongside the biblical narrative.

Fourthly, in seeking to orientate the listener to the biblical text, it is helpful to consider re-telling the text's story in the active present-tense voice. The goal is to achieve immediacy of perspective so the listener joins the preacher in becoming a first-hand witness to that which is transpiring. Note, in this regard it is not that the bridegroom *arrived*, but rather that the bridegroom *is arriving*. Listeners are caught in the electrifying energy of the moment as they become part of the crowd that waits to enter into the great wedding banquet. By the simple turning of verbs from the past to present-tense voice, listeners have opportunity to be part of the on-site reporting team now delivering the text's breaking news reports. For too long, preachers have held listeners at a distance to the text, without even realizing this has been the case. We have been required to view ancient words through antiquated theological telescopes. While we may have the ability to zoom in on certain truths, how much more effective our experience would be if we could walk the same road Jesus walked and stand in the crowd among those who first heard Jesus' teaching. Preaching that effectively seeks to orientate the listener to the text and aims to recreate active first-hand engagement. In so doing, both preacher and listener alike are able to link their testimony together to say, "We have seen the Lord!"

Strategy #2—Textual Disorientation

Within the second section of the sermon manuscript, the primary goal is to identify what is strange and unsettling about the text. What does not make sense? What speed bumps do we encounter? What seems out of place? In this space of sermonic development, preachers have opportunity to push the boundaries of the text to identify what actually pushes back at them.

In the case of the Parable of the Wise and Foolish Bridesmaids, there is a sense in which we readily see that this is not your average wedding story. We can imagine some poor wedding planner scrambling madly to redeem that which is falling apart in terms of scheduling and planning. Pushing the boundaries of the text further, we notice other unsettling details. For instance, why is there so much attention given to a bridegroom and no reference by Matthew to a bride? Who starts a wedding reception at the midnight hour? What do we make of a bridegroom who so ruthlessly casts out the foolish bridesmaids, just because they ran a little short on oil for their lamps? When we link the bridegroom's role in the story to be representative of Christ, how will we reconcile this picture of unrelenting judgment?

In working these tensions of the text, the goal is for the listener to experience the bodily weight of truth. Thomas Troeger, in *Imagining a Sermon*, gives emphasis to this when he speaks about how "truth that matters to us has a physical impact on our bodies ... our stomachs knot, our fists clinch, our shoulders bend under the burden. But whether joyful or saddening, truth ... has a bodily weight, a physical force on our animal frames."[4] As *disorientation* evolves in the second part of the sermon, the preacher works to cultivate within the listener some form of physical response. Perhaps we will want to pound on the door with the foolish bridesmaids, crying out, "This judgment is unfair. Give us more time! Give us a second chance." Maybe we will want to affirm the reaction of the bridegroom or shake the foolish girls for not figuring out their circumstances earlier. Whatever we work to accomplish in *disorientation*, the goal is that the listeners would sit in the centre of textual tensions and begin actively trying to navigate their way over the imposing speed bumps before them.

Preachers will be helped further in this section of the sermon to give some thought as to what an alternate screenplay might look like for the text. For instance, if the parable did not play out as it did, what alternate scripts might we imagine? Imagine the bridegroom arriving. The foolish bridesmaids make their confession that they have run out of oil. The bridegroom says, "No problem, ladies. I know that you have been diligently waiting here all night. I know your intentions were good. We will not worry about this small oversight. Come on into the party and we will just pretend this did not happen." While the bridegroom could have made this response, Matthew says, he did not. By playing out this alternate screenplay in the sermon, listeners move deeper into the text's tension. Naturally, listeners begin to ask, "Why didn't the bridegroom make that response? Why was grace absent in this final moment of judgment? Why did the bridegroom not provide a second chance?

Similarly, we might play an alternate screenplay with our focus turned toward the wise bridesmaids. As the foolish bridesmaids come to them asking for a loan of oil for their lamps, imagine if instead of rejecting the foolish girls' request that the wise girls accommodated. They say, "No problem, take some of our oil. It may mean we will not make it into the banquet because there may not be enough for the both of us. But here, take some of what we have and let's hope we can stay our course." In the end, no one enters the banquet, because no one has enough oil. While a total blackout happens around this wedding feast, the bridegroom stands alone with no one to attend the banquet. Note in this scenario that if we lift the faithful stewardship of the wise bridesmaids out of the story we lose a valuable teaching element. We need the witness of the wise bridesmaids to remind us how we are to cultivate a heart of preparation for the bridegroom's return. This alternate screenplay pushes us closer to seeing the valued role the wise bridesmaids actually play in pressing the parable's main point.

In all that takes place in this section of the sermon, the ultimate goal is to name that which is disturbing and unsettling to the listener. We do not particularly like the way this wedding story plays out. There does not seem to be the possibility of a "happily-ever-after ending," especially for the foolish bridesmaids. We will struggle to reconcile our perspective of God's grace and compassion with a God who seems to slam the door in the face of those who, in the moment, are seeking their way into the kingdom. Naming these harsh realities will not only do much to enliven preaching, but it will assist listeners in opening their imagination to new possibilities. In so doing, our strategy in identifying what is disturbing and disorientating in the text achieves a similar outcome of disturbing and disorientating the hearts and minds of those engaging the text. This opens an effective space for preaching a disturbing gospel because listeners have found their own way into the biblical story.

Strategy #3—Textual Re-orientation

In the third and final section of the sermon, the preacher makes an intentional move to glue the fragmented (disorientated) pieces of the text back together. In this regard, the preacher works to define two important elements, the first being the theological tension that exists in the text. At this point the preacher asks such questions as: What picture of God is evolving? How does this sit in relationship with what we know to be true about the nature and will of the Holy One? Where do we see points of conflict? Where do we see the text pushing us to navigate new horizons of theological thought?

Secondly, the preacher will work to define what is true of the text's rhetorical impact. To do this, the preacher must ultimately answer, "What is the text doing?" What impact is the text having upon the listener? Thomas Long, in *Preaching and the Literary Forms of the Bible*, offers excellent insight into this element when he says that every genre of text has some kind of impact or effect upon a typical reader or hearer. For example, a joke is a genre designed to make us laugh. A riddle causes us to think in certain oblique ways. A ghost story can frighten us. Texts have the capacity to exercise a powerful guiding influence over the willing and careful reader.[5] After the preacher has grappled with the content and flow of the story by pushing and pulling at that which is unsettling, the preacher must then ask what this text is working to accomplish. What impact did the text have on its first audience? What impact does it have today? Is the text inspiring faith, motivating commitment or engendering a longing to grow closer to Christ? Maybe the text creates a burden of guilt and pushes the listener toward a desire for mercy and forgiveness. Perhaps the text creates a restlessness to become more engaged in acts of service or invites listeners to align themselves more deliberately with the values of the kingdom. Whatever the intended outcome, in the re-orientation stage of this sermon model the preacher works diligently to name what the text is doing in its original context and then to align this with the purposes of the sermon.

In the case of the Parable of the Wise and Foolish Bridesmaids, the preacher leaves the text holding both the weight and the wonder of the gospel message. We feel the burden of those who have failed to find their way into the great wedding banquet. Our ears still reverberate with the sound of doors slamming and foolish young girls pounding at the entrance for a second chance. The weight of this message is pronounced. Yet also, a sense of wonder grips us as the text draws us toward its ultimate expression of testimony. We offer our thanksgiving, for we see a picture of a God who is faithful to execute his judgment in order that there might be fulfilment to his promises. The final shutting of the door marks the beginning of the eternal life God has promised. Therefore, let us trim our wicks and be ready for the arrival of the bridegroom, for the door is still open. All who desire access to this promise can still find the way.

Strategy #4—Creating Focus and Function Statements

After a succinct outline has been developed, incorporating the elements previously named, and before the preacher moves to the final manuscript, it is critical for the preacher to review where he or she is heading with sermon development. What key statements will form the sermon's focus? In one sentence, can the preacher name what the sermon will be about? Too often, preachers rush toward their manuscripts with ideas overflowing, without establishing a clear road map as to where preaching ideas will land. To assist in formulating this plan, clear focus and function statements will need to be established. While these may evolve in earlier stages of exegesis, the point is that before writing the sermon, these statements need to be well defined. Note: we highlight the need for these statements, not to further burden the preacher's sermon process, but to ensure that continuity of focus is achieved and that the sermon arrives at its intended destination. Thomas Long, in *The Witness of Preaching*, defines these terms and presses the importance of preachers articulating these points of reference before preaching:

A focus statement is a concise description of the central controlling and unifying theme of the sermon. In short, this is what the whole of the sermon will be "about."

A function statement is a description of what the preacher hopes the sermon will create or cause to happen for the hearers. Sermons make demands upon the hearers, which is another way of saying that they provoke change in the hearers (even if the change is a deepening of something already present). The function statement names the hoped-for change.[6]

This will undoubtedly become the hardest part of the homiletical process, as preachers force themselves to grapple with the specifics of their language for preaching. Long emphasizes how important it is that these statements grow out of the experience of studying the biblical text and that both focus and function statements have relationship to each other. When these are fully achieved, preachers are ready to begin formalizing a manuscript for preaching. Preachers are encouraged, however, to remember the importance of using language intentionally so that words will not be wasted, but that every element included in the sermon will push toward the desired outcome.

Conclusion

The parables of the New Testament provide an excellent framework from which contemporary preachers can work to proclaim the unsettling news of a disturbing gospel. Three primary strategies will guide this process as attention focuses toward orientation, disorientation and re-orientation. Orientation will serve to open up a general way for the listeners to enter into the text where they can determine their location and begin to take in a detailed tour of what the text has to offer. Disorientation will work systematically to name what is disturbing or unsettling to the listeners' frame of reference as they enter the strangeness of the biblical text's world. By intentionally engaging textual speed bumps, listeners press naturally toward theological tensions and wrestle with these on their own terms. Re-orientation systematically works to draw fragmented pieces back into a whole, with the intent of using rhetorical impact (what the text is doing) to shape the design and structure of the sermon. In short, the preacher works to mirror what the text is doing within the body of the sermon. If the text is inspiring faith, so should the sermon. If the text is confronting injustice, so should the sermon. If the text is enlivening hope, so should the sermon. Note: in these points of reference, the preacher works to use strong verbs to articulate the action of the text. It is not just that the text informs, explains or enlightens, although these responses may all be representative of what is going on in a given text. Rather, it is recognizing that the Word of God is reaching out to listeners with holy energy and divine power. While biblical texts may impart information and explain complex doctrine, the bigger issue is how the text assimilates the response of both the head and the heart. In so doing, we ask what is enlivened or awakened within those sitting in the pews? Preachers who effectively navigate these elements press closer to effectively preaching what is both gripping and gloriously true of the disturbing gospel we proclaim.

Finally, preachers are encouraged to evaluate whether they have formulated concise focus and function statements to give the sermon a logical sense of forward momentum and purpose. In so doing, preachers recognize that their words have the power to arrest the attention of hopeless sinners (to whom we are all kin) to bring a message that is life-giving and new. How important it is then that when the sermon launches out of the gate it is moving forward toward the listener and has in clear view its final destination. To clarify further the details of this chapter, sample sermons follow so that readers might see how both parabolic and non-parabolic texts can effectively embrace the orientation/disorientation/re-orientation model for preaching. Further reading resources are recommended in Appendix E for those who desire to take this study deeper.

SAMPLE SERMON

LOCKED OUT AND NOWHERE TO GO

Text: Matthew 25:1-13
The Parable of the Wise and Foolish Bridesmaids

Focus Statement: Christ calls us to live in both the weightiness and wonder of the gospel message.

Function Statement: This sermon will seek to lead listeners into the strangeness of the biblical parable, while intentionally inviting them to embrace the weightiness and wonder of the gospel message for themselves.

Homiletical Strategy: This sermon launches the theme of preparing for the Second Coming of Christ with the humorous recounting of a Y2K story. This is intentionally used as it represents an accessible place of memory for the audience. A move is then made to **orient** the listener to the biblical text, establishing prior context to the parable. A simple retelling of the story follows, leaving listeners with the slamming sound of the closed door reverberating in their ears.

A second move is made toward **disorientation**. What is strange and unsettling about this wedding story? Here, deliberate care is taken to not name all of the puzzling elements that have come out of a study of the text. Focus centres primarily on the harshness of a bridegroom that shuts the foolish bridesmaids out. While more attention could be given to allegorical interpretation, the only reference this sermon will make in this light is that the bridegroom, in Matthew's mind, represents Christ. (Concern here is to avoid creating a complexity of sermon layers and to keep the message focused and simple.)

A third move is made toward **re-orientation**, acknowledging how the closed door to the kingdom is a symbol of both the gospel's weightiness and its wonder. Herein lies the hope of this text and the need for the listeners to concretely consider their response.

Introduction:

At the turn of the millennium, the world faced the unforgiving deadline of December 31, 1999. Great fear and uncertainty loomed in the arena of technology as computer gurus sought to determine how they could come at the Y2K bug. If you recall, the primary issue was the uncertainty of what would happen when computer clocks turned over to the year 2000. Would technology read the triple zero in the year or would it revert to the year 1900?

Predictions went forth of worldwide havoc. Experts warned of the grounding of airplanes, the shutdown of oil, gas and water stations, country-wide power outages, bank machine failure and food shortages. Doomsayers said, "The end is coming; prepare to meet your God!"

Maclean's magazine, at the time, ran an article about the Eckhart family from Lisbon, Ohio. Bruce Eckhart was one who was convinced the problem would not be fixed in time and so he started implementing a Y2K survival plan for his family. For more than a year, he began storing up food in his basement. He purchased two rifles, a shotgun and a handgun to fight off the unprepared. He converted his home to a gas-powered generator. Finally, he bought their 11-year-old daughter, Danielle, a waterbed. In a pinch they'd always have an extra 1,000 litres on hand! From time to time Bruce would run surprise Y2K drills. He'd shut down the power, fire up the generator, run through the house blowing a whistle and shouting, "Y2K is here!" Then he would count how many appliances the generator would handle. With his basement lined with boxes of canned chow mein and dehydrated beans, this was a man who was intent on being prepared for the end.

Orientation:

As we come to Matthew's Gospel, Chapter 24, we encounter another story about preparation for end times. As we parachute into this parable about the wise and foolish bridesmaids, we discover the story itself is part of a larger theology lecture Jesus is giving to his disciples. As we arrive in Chapter 24 in the Mount of Olives, we are a little late for the class. The question sitting at the centre of the circle is this: "Master, when will we know the end of the age? What will be the sign of your coming?" (Matthew 24:3). Jesus has a tough task to try and help his disciples get their minds around this one. And so he begins by talking about rumours of wars and earthquakes, famines, false prophets, increase in lawlessness and times of great suffering. "But hold on," says Jesus. "Even though all those things may be happening, the end is still not yet!" "Stay awake," says Jesus. "Keep alert for no one knows the exact day or the hour; only the Father. Therefore you must be ready for the Son of Man is coming at an unexpected hour" (Matthew 24:42, 44).

I think Jesus realized at that point, he had some learning challenges in the crowd. And so Jesus says: In case you are having trouble picturing this, let me tell you a story. For the kingdom of heaven will be like 10 bridesmaids who take their lamps and go out to meet the bridegroom. Five wise maids anticipate the fact that the bridegroom may be delayed and so they take their lamps and some extra oil to be prepared for the long wait. Five, however, are foolish. They think they know exactly when the bridegroom is going to show. They have their watches set and so they have no contingency plan. They take their lamps but have no extra oil. Sure enough, the bridegroom is delayed! All of the maids become drowsy and fall asleep. But at the midnight hour, text messages are going off in every corner; cellphones are ringing! Outside the door a loud voice is heard shouting—"Here is the bridegroom. Come out and meet him." The bridesmaids get up to trim their lamps, and it's then the foolish bridesmaids realize, "Oh no! Houston—we have a problem! We are going to need some oil for these lamps.

"And how hard will this be? Let's just borrow some from the other girls. After all—they are our friends. They won't need everything they've got." Simple solution! Well—not really! For in a rather unexpected twist, the wise bridesmaids are not so willing to share their resources. Perhaps their solution is to go check out the corner convenience store; maybe they will have some oil they can buy there. While these foolish maids head off to take care of business, the wise bridesmaids go out to meet the bridegroom and because they are ready—because they are prepared—they enter into the celebration of the banquet. The door to the kingdom closes behind them.

Later on, the other bridesmaids come knocking on the door, (25:11) saying, "Lord, Lord, open to us." But the bridegroom replies, "Truly I tell you, I do not know you. You don't have a relationship with me! You have missed the time of my coming. And so now you are locked out of the kingdom!" As the sentence of darkness falls, we know from Matthew this is not a desirable place, but a place where there will be weeping and gnashing of teeth.

Disorientation:

Well, I don't know about you, but Matthew doesn't impress me much with his ability to tell a good wedding story! Not good material here for the Learning Channel's next up-and-coming episode of *A Wedding Story*! After all, where is the sense of romance—the pageantry, the magic and an ending that says they drove off into the sunset and lived happily ever after?

In fact, if we push the boundaries of this text a little further, we realize there are a number of unsettling elements in this story. For instance, whoever heard of a wedding without a bride? Why is there so much attention focused on the bridegroom? Who starts a wedding reception in the middle of the night? Why isn't there a wedding planner on the scene co-ordinating things a little more successfully? What are we to make of this bridegroom, who in the end shows no mercy or compassion for the bridesmaids who come late and unprepared? Why isn't there forgiveness? Why isn't there opportunity for a second chance? Isn't that what the gospel of grace is supposed to be all about?

It's at this point in the sermon the preacher says—maybe we should find a different text for the Sunday sermon! This is a hard story to tell! If we could have words this morning with Matthew, maybe we'd tell him that this picture of a ruthless unrelenting, unsympathetic, unforgiving bridegroom is hard to take in, especially when we recognize that when Matthew speaks about the bridegroom, he's really speaking about Christ.

And so what are we to do with this picture of Christ? What are we to do with the Christ who once said, "I am the door; no one enters except by me" (John 10:7)? Here we are in Matthew's Gospel trying to gain entrance at the door, but we can't get in. Yes, we admit it! We've been a little off our game! Yes, we are coming late! Yes, maybe we all aren't the brightest crayons in the box! We should have been more prepared. But doesn't it count that we are here now? Here we stand pleading our case, begging for mercy, longing for understanding, but there is no forgiveness. There is no leniency. There is no grace. What is Jesus really inviting us to see?

Re-orientation:

As we struggle with the question, we sit ourselves down on the front steps of the bridegroom's home. The darkness closes in. We listen to the agonizing of the foolish maids: Why didn't we listen? Why didn't we get the oil when we had time? Why didn't we recognize the time of the bridegroom's coming? Why didn't we take this more seriously?

In this moment, we realize that *we have encountered both the weightiness and the wonder of the gospel message.* For yes, there is coming a day when Jesus will return and the door will be shut to those who are unprepared. That's the weighted harsh reality of the kingdom of God. But the wonder that the gospel tells us is that when that day comes there will be an end to pain and suffering in our world: darkness will be as light, healing will come to the nations, peace will reign over all the earth, and the perfect kingdom that God has promised will be realized. The fact that the door will finally be shut points to the sure foundation of this word. The shutting of the door is the final seal on God's promises. It's the final amen that says, "It's finished—the battle is over. Jesus Christ shall reign as Lord for ever and ever."

So we have a choice this morning—whether we will live in the weightiness of the gospel message or the wonder. While one day the door will be shut, right now the door is open! God, in his mercy, gives us this moment in time to make sure our lamps are well oiled. We are not a people doomed to the fate of eternal suffering and damnation. We are not a people who necessarily have to bear this sentence of judgment and darkness. God has provided a way of escape through the cross of Jesus Christ. As we acknowledge and confess the things in our lives that separate us from God and as we open ourselves to the forgiveness and mercy of God, we can be rescued from the fate of the closed door.

And so Matthew invites us to hold up a mirror to this parable. Perhaps many of us see our own reflection. We have lulled ourselves into thinking there will always be more time to go out and buy the oil; more time to make changes in our lives; more time to reconcile differences; more time to make an apology; more time to get serious about being the kind of disciple Christ calls us to be; more time to let our light shine.

While we could get stuck on the weightiness of the closed door, Jesus wants us to see the wonder of the open door. For the kingdom of heaven is one day going to host the most amazing reception we could ever imagine. Every one of us, without exception, is invited. Everyone one of us can have a place with the bridegroom. So we keep watch and alert, storing up our canned chow mein, our dehydrated beans, and, oh yes, we definitely won't forget the oil! Amen.

SAMPLE SERMON

LOAVES-AND-FISHES MOMENTS

Text: Luke 9:10-17
Jesus Feeds the Five Thousand

Focus Statement: Jesus invites us to place him continually in the centre of all our problems.

Function Statement: The intent of this sermon is to move listeners to their own loaves-and-fishes moment where they might actively respond to lessons of faith.

Homiletical Strategy: This sermon was preached initially as part of a series entitled, "I-Witness News", which focused on varying New Testament miracle accounts. The introduction sets listeners up to think about moments in their lives where problem-solving strategies have been required. A second move within the introduction presses this toward the lived experiences of the intended audience. For it can be hard to remember the lessons of faith when faced with the hard realities of our lives.

Under **orientation**, the sermon moves to open up the biblical story with specific focus toward the disciples' struggle to know how to meet the physical needs of the 5,000 people standing before them. Note: Specific emphasis is given in this section to drawing in contemporary ways in which any one of us might come at the problem. A second move is made in this section to intensify the identification of our own struggle to call up the lessons of faith through the inclusion of the statement: sometimes it is hard to problem-solve in remote places.

Disorientation begins as the sermon begins to unpack the significant speed bumps in the text that come primarily through the disciples' response: "Let's go buy them some food." Drawing in contemporary references and images, the goal is to give the listener the ability to see the complexity of the situation unfolding through the lens of human struggle.

The final **re-orientation** section of the sermon glues the textual picture back together by calling listeners to see the lesson Jesus has had on the blackboard since the very first day of class: "Put me in the centre of your problems and we will work things out together."

The sermon concludes with examples of loaves-and-fishes moments that would have been in the recent memory of the audience. This final move reminds the preacher of the importance of identifying God's active work in the midst of those to whom we preach. We are God's finest "I-Witness" reporters!

Introduction:

I found myself in an interesting predicament a few weeks ago. It was about 10:00 p.m. in the evening. I am driving home from music rehearsals at the church. I pull in the driveway and push the button inside the van to open up the garage door, only to discover that it's not working like it normally does! So I hit the pad again, thinking maybe it just didn't connect. Still no response! So I try again … still no open door. After about five or six attempts, I start to register that something isn't quite right. So then I start working my options. I get out of the van and use my key to go in the side door of the garage. I hit the pad inside to see if that would open things up. Still nothing, but this time I hear the groaning sound of the door motor telling me that things aren't sounding so good! I don't know if I am in denial or what it is—but I give it another try. I press the button; I press it some more. I'm saying to myself—this door has to work! All of sudden, as if there had never been an issue, the door goes up with no problem. I give a big sigh of relief. Thank you, Lord—problem solved. I drive the van into its space, push the pad again and the door closes.

But as I'm walking out of the garage, all of a sudden I hear these haunting voices: Julie, maybe you should just try that one more time to make sure it's going to open OK for the morning. So back I go. I put my hand to the push pad and … nothing! No winding motor sound; no lifting door. And now my van is a hostage to my garage with no possible means of escape! What to do? I have children who have to be driven to school early the next morning; I have appointments to keep; I need my vehicle on the street, not locked up in my garage. I have a problem. I need to solve this problem. I need a solution to this problem and I need it in a hurry, because the implications of this situation are feeling a little overwhelming in the moment.

As I share that story, I am conscious that trying to solve the problem of broken garage doors pales in comparison to some of the problems people in our world have to solve today. In the complexity and messiness of life, finding solutions to our problems can sometimes be very overwhelming. Sometimes when problems come, it's hard to think clearly! A teenage daughter comes and tells a parent she's pregnant; your boss tells you you're being laid off; a member of your family walks away from faith, saying they want nothing more to do with the church; your doctor gives you the tests results and it's not what you expected. It's not what you hoped for. Sometimes it's hard to work through life's problems, in both their simplest and most complex forms. Sometimes it's hard to remember the lessons of faith that are supposed to help us make sense of the moment and carry us through!

Orientation:

I wonder if this was something of the disciples' experience in the passage we read earlier from Luke 9:10-17. As the disciples register the reality of their situation, it seems hard to remember the lessons of faith. Here they are in this remote place on the northern shore of the Sea of Galilee. This is not one of your more popular tourist destinations. Yet there they are doing ministry with Jesus; even though it was just supposed to be something of a retreat for Jesus and the disciples. Chances are, however, there had to have been good media coverage that day or at least good communication via word of mouth. For on this occasion, Jesus ends up attracting more than 5,000 people to hear his message. Jesus spends the day teaching about the kingdom of God and healing the sick. It's been a good day in ministry. But now it's getting late. The afternoon light is almost gone. The disciples start to register the reality of their situation. Soon this crowd is going to be saying, "We're hungry, Where can we get something to eat around here?" Soon they're going to need a place to sleep, all 5,000 of them. And when was the last time any of us ever tried to make hotel reservations for more than 5,000 people? When was the last time any of us tried to rustle up a few leftovers to feed that kind of a crowd? We have no on-line connections to check out available accommodations in Bethsaida; the disciples register their reality ... and they struggle to remember the lessons of faith.

In verse 12, they finally go to Jesus and say, "Master, we've got a situation developing here. Here's what you need to do! You need to send this crowd away now so they can go to the surrounding villages and countryside and find food and lodging, because we are in a remote place." We don't have a lot of options for problem-solving here.

Last summer we found ourselves in a similar situation. We were driving the Trans-Canada Highway in southern Saskatchewan's remote prairie land. All along the way, we are taking careful note of where the next gas stations are. We pass a sign that says: Next service station 45 kilometres. I look at my husband. He looks at me. No problem, we'll make it! About a half hour later, we have to register reality: we are not going to make the 45 kilometres remaining. The gas gauge is getting very low, with all the head winds we had experienced. It is time to fuel up—but there's no service to be found, except maybe in one of these off-the-beaten-track prairie communities. So off the highway we go into this tiny prairie community. There are two houses, and two elderly men sitting outside in their pickup truck talking. We pull up alongside. We roll down the window. "Anywhere around here to get gas?" we say. These fellows scratch their heads. "Hmmm," they say. "Mikey up the hill; he might keep some in his garage from when he used to fix lawn mowers! You could give him a try!" So we make our way up the hill. Needless to say, Mikey who used to fix lawnmowers didn't have the gas and we probably made it on fumes the rest of the way down the road. *When we have to solve problems in remote places, sometimes, this can be a hard thing!* Sometimes "remote" comes through our feelings of loneliness, abandonment or just the strangeness of the unfamiliar road we are being forced to travel. When faced with the reality of our problems, sometimes it's hard to see the possibilities and it's hard to call up the lessons of faith.

Disorientation:

Jesus has but one solution to offer to this reality that is presenting itself to the disciples. He looks them square in the eyes and says: "Boys! You give them something to eat! You solve this problem!"

I can only imagine the look that must have flashed across their faces: "Us? Us—give them something to eat. Listen, Jesus, the best we can come up with here is five loaves of bread. Count them, Jesus: one, two, three, four, five. That's—well, do the math; that's roughly one loaf of bread for every thousand people! And over here, we've got no more than two fish! Not sure, Jesus, this is really going to fly here! Unless, well, here's an idea ... we could go out and buy something for this crowd!"

And it's right there in that moment of Luke's rendering of this story, we have first-hand evidence that these disciples don't get it! While recognizing their reality, they are failing to call up the lessons of faith. They are not thinking too clearly in the moment. Here, Jesus has yet one more teaching opportunity with the Twelve. Yes, they have a problem; yes, they need a solution; yes, they need it in a hurry. But going out to buy food; how was that going to work? What corner store at the intersection of nowhere and nowhere is going to have enough provisions to feed more than 5,000 people? What remote community is going to have even a pizza service that can deliver for this kind of crowd? Think about it. If, at best, an extra-large pizza could feed six to eight people, we'd need approximately 833 pizzas, and that's only feeding the men in the crowd! We still have to add in the women and children! Or what desert remote place can instantly produce caterers to take on a meal for this multitude? Shall we just call out for a KFC buffet or maybe Chinese take-out, anyone? Where might we reasonably think we could buy this food?

Then add into this story one other significant speed bump. Look back to what Luke tells us in verse 3 of this chapter. Because here is another reality! Jesus has commissioned these disciples to declare their complete solidarity with the poor and to place their total trust in Christ to provide for their needs. Verse 3: these disciples aren't traveling with any money. Jesus says, "Take nothing for the journey; no staff, no bag, no bread, no money and no extra tunic." So whose budget is going to pay for this brainy idea to "buy food for the masses"? What fund are we going to take this out of, if we have one at all?

Now overwhelmed by the responsibility that is being thrust upon them, the disciples register their reality, but fail to apply the lesson of faith.

Re-orientation:

In this moment of the story, Jesus seeks to teach a lesson that has been on the blackboard from the very first day of classes! Jesus is saying to trust him to provide what is needed. Put him in the centre of this problem and let him work this out with you.

So the teaching moment unfolds. At Jesus' command, the disciples divide the crowd into groups of 50. (Notice they do not argue with Jesus about this; they know Jesus' track record; they know something extraordinary is about to happen.) Verse 16: taking the loaves and the two fish, looking up to heaven, he gives thanks and breaks the bread. Then he gives the food to the disciples to pass out to the people. Everyone eats; everyone is satisfied; and there's more tuna-fish sandwiches left over than any one of us could imagine! As Jesus is placed at the centre of the problem, he pours out his power, and every need present that day is met in Christ and in Christ alone. Here again is the lesson of faith! When we are faced with difficult realities, *when we have to problem-solve in remote places, Jesus calls us to remember the lessons of faith and to put him at the centre of our circumstances.*

We don't have to be in the remote region of Bethsaida following in the footsteps of the disciples to know that Jesus is alive and actively working in our world. Loaves-and-fishes moments still happen in the places where you and I live. It was true in Bathurst, New Brunswick, on Wednesday, January 16, 2008, when more than 5,000 people gathered to say farewell to seven young basketball players who were victims of a tragic road crash. As their names were called out in the service, the officiating clergy said, "Think of these young men with hope and faith; for they do not belong to death, they belong to Jesus Christ. For it is from the light of Jesus Christ we draw our strength and our vision to move forward when the darkness befalls us." You see, I think that was a kind of loaves-and-fishes moment. Jesus is being brought into the centre of the picture. Jesus is being brought into all that pain and heartache. Jesus Christ was ministering his grace to hurting, broken people.

We saw it right here in Winnipeg last Tuesday. Lisa Klassen's SUV plunges over the guardrail of a North Perimeter Bridge and spirals into the Red River. Yet God is in the centre of that reality. God sends his rescuers. And we've heard wonderful words of testimony from this family as they have spoken about their faith and the strength they draw from Christ. Again it's a loaves-and-fishes moment. God is being brought into the centre of this reality and God's people trust him in the moment. What are some of the things in your life to which God is saying, "Trust me; just depend on me"?

Let us again today confirm and reaffirm the lesson of the loaves and the fishes. Let us throw ourselves into the wideness of God's mercy and the fullness of Christ's love where there will always be abundance for us all, and the table will never be empty; but with Christ, we will always be filled.

SAMPLE SERMON

AT THE RIVER'S EDGE

Text: Exodus 2:1-10
A Baby in the Bulrushes

Focus Statement: Our experience of God in the darkness of life circumstances invites us to identify his continuing divine activity in our lives.

Function Statement: The intent of this sermon is to enliven faith in the listener to identify the continuing activity of God in their circumstances.

Homiletical Strategy: Using the **orientation/disorientation/ re-orientation** model for preaching, this sermon seeks to demonstrate how this approach accommodates Old Testament narrative texts. Within the introduction, effort is made to lead listeners toward a sense of "riverbank" where they are invited to reflect upon what they see.

Moving to **orientate** the listener to the text, the main emphasis of this section is to emphasize how those gathered by the riverbank of the text struggle to see God's presence in the text. Note that this is not directly named by the author but is developed from the action of the narrative.

Within the **disorientation** stage of the sermon, the hard theological question is engaged. Why does God allow the suffering of such innocence? A brief alternate screenplay is used to suggest ways in which God could be mediating the situation, but is obviously choosing not to. Pressing toward the listener's own expression of experience, the question plays out as to why God can't just wave a magic wand and fix all the unjust circumstances of our lives.

Using these foundational thoughts, the sermon finally moves to **re-orientation** to identify the opportunities we have at the river's edge to rejoice in the work that God is doing in our midst. While there may not be neon lights flashing and brass bands playing, we will know the work of God if we have been to the river and viewed our circumstances through the lens of faith.

Introduction:

Growing up as a dairy farmer's daughter, living way out in the country, seldom seemed to have too many advantages. While my girlfriends in town spent time at the mall and the movies, I was out riding on the back of a tractor, helping my dad with farm work.

If there was one advantage to my rural upbringing, it was the simple fact that it kept us close to nature. My most favourite place on the farm was across the cornfield, down by the river. When my brother and I had completed our chores, we would often make our way down to the river. We would tell my mom that we were just going to skip some rocks. She would skeptically send us on our way with a warning. "Make sure you stay out of the water!" she would say. We would dutifully reply—"Yes, Mom, we promise; we'll stay dry. No worries!"

Nine times out of 10, however, we would come home, soaking wet, despite our mother's warnings. As we would sneak around the corner of the house, Mom would be there, hands on hips. Her familiar line would follow. *"And what do I see here?"* she would say. Those memorable days at the river usually had consequences. Yet, it did not stop us from going back, over and over again.

Orientation:

Today our text from Exodus 2:1-10 invites us to the river's edge. As we stand on the bank of the Nile, *(writing to the senses)* we feel the gentle breeze blowing across the water. We can hear the sound of the wind stirring through the bulrushes. Here, the writer of this text subtly asks us: *"What do you see here?"* What is on our viewfinder as we scan this setting? Along the riverbank, we notice (*use of present tense*) the approach of a rather intriguing entourage. In fact, it's a royal entourage! The Pharaoh's daughter is getting ready to take a swim. According to verse 5 of our text (*intentional reference to the text*) her attendants are walking alongside the riverbank with her. Perhaps they are scouting out the presence of the paparazzi who are lurking somewhere in the wings trying to get their scoop for the royal tabloids. Perhaps some assist the princess as she gets in and out of the water. Perhaps she has a personal trainer timing her laps. Other attendants stand guard, watching that no one intrudes on these private moments.

All of a sudden, the sound of a crying baby interrupts the order of this scene. Our eyes fall upon a floating basket caught among the reeds. Something in this picture is not quite right. The princess sends her slave girl to fetch this basket. When she opens the basket, we realize our ears have not deceived us. We have heard the cry of a helpless baby. Very quickly the Pharaoh's daughter identifies that it is a Hebrew baby.

As that word "Hebrew" suspends itself in the air, all of a sudden we realize we may need more information to really understand what is going on here. Since we have no online access down by the river, we cannot "Google" this word "Hebrew." We can only rely upon that which echoes in our ears from other texts (*focus toward listening to the echoes of Scripture*). We have heard about Hebrew babies before. In Exodus 1:16, 22, the Pharaoh himself gave explicit orders that all male Hebrew babies were to be killed and thrown into the Nile River. The King feared that the Israelites were becoming too numerous. If war was to come, the king agonized that an army would rise up underneath him, fight against him and leave the country. No king ever wants to be in a position such as this.

Male Hebrew babies are those trapped alongside their Hebrew parents, Hebrew sisters and Hebrew families. They are helpless to change their societal position. They are children of slaves without power or privilege. We are now plunged into their world of danger and desperation. On our viewfinder, we try to adjust the light metre because there is a darkness that hovers. This riverbank is an empty place, devoid of hope or expectation. There are no pro-life protestors demanding justice here for the oppressed. Life for an innocent child, "hangs by a thread," as a helpless mother and a lone sister struggle by this riverbank.

Disorientation:

Understanding these tensions, we step just a little bit closer to the river's edge. As we watch a baby floating by in a basket, we say, "God, why would you allow the suffering of such innocence *(alternate screenplay)*? Why, God, are you not marching in with tanks and battalions to take this Pharaoh out of the picture? Why are you not at least trying to infiltrate this situation with secret service agents? Why God? Can't you work to put a more righteous ruler on the throne? How could we ever get to this place where a mother truly feels she has no option but to give in to this injustice and to hand her child over to this river of death? Why is it, God, you seem so absent from this riverbank?"

(*Trying to press toward listener's world; need element*) As we ask these questions, perhaps something echoes within us. For how often in our lives have we stood at the river's edge feeling the weight of life's burdens upon us; or feeling the impossibility of our predicaments? Perhaps, it's our struggle when an unexpected eviction notice is plastered to our door. It's what we feel when we hear the doctor's words, "We are sorry—we did all that we could." Perhaps it is the question that roars through our minds walking away from the job with pink slip in hand, not knowing how next week's rent will be paid.

We say, "Why God? Why do you seem so absent? Why can't you just wave your magic wand and fix all this trouble in our world?" (*Note here the preacher has chosen to create pictures; another option is to include an actual story that depicts truth.*)

Re-orientation:

So we must decide. **What do we see at this river's edge?** Just when we think it is only about hopelessness, death and despair, all of a sudden an incredible plot unfolds. Flashing back we see how this mother prepares her child for the river. We see how she carefully coats the basket with tar and pitch. She makes it waterproof. She does all she can to give her child a fighting chance. She creates her own miniature floating ark. Maybe the Pharaoh subsequently wished he'd added some fine print to his original edict. Notice that no one said anything about how these babies were to be thrown into the river! Notice there are no guidelines or policies; no protocols or prescriptions; no specific plan! So the mother devises a plan—it just happens to be a plan devised and mediated by God himself. It's a God plan!

Off in the distance, the baby's sister hovers; guarding; protecting; waiting anxiously to see what might happen. When the Pharaoh's daughter makes her discovery, the sister moves in. Before we know it, she's negotiated an adoption plan that puts this baby right back in his mother's arms! When the child is grown—one that was originally condemned by the Pharaoh—he becomes a grandson of the royal court! As we stand at the river's edge, we say, "These things don't just happen! This has to be the work of God!" So let's get ready for the service of celebration! Let's get ready to give God the glory for this successful rescue operation. For surely God has to get the credit for all of this! Only a powerful, almighty, all-knowing, creating, life-giving God *(note accumulation of descriptors!)* can deliver these kinds of miracles. You don't have to be an Einstein to figure out what is going on here. God's footprints are all over this riverbank. God is redeeming his people; God is fulfilling his promises; God is carrying out his divine plan. God is conquering evil. God is giving life! *(Repetition of theo-centric driven sentences!)*

There is just one problem. No one here by the river is giving God any credit! There is no reference to God anywhere in this story. No word spoken by God! No physical appearance made by God. In fact, God is silent. God doesn't seem to be calling for the party. Some might try to tell us God is invisible. From our vantage point by the river, we want to say to this biblical narrator, "Wake up here! You are missing an incredible teaching moment!" This is the time to break out the banners and the bands and neon flashing signs. This is a time to parade through the streets proclaiming, "LOOK WHAT GOD HAS

DONE! TO GOD BE THE GLORY, GREAT THINGS HE HAS DONE." God's rescue mission has been successful! A Hebrew baby has been saved! God is raising up a leader to liberate his people. A plan has been initiated to overcome injustice. Yet for some reason the text is silent on this particular matter. We have to ask, what was this writer's point? Toward what are we being directed? What do we see by this river's edge?

In the end, perhaps it is as simple as this. The biblical writer says, "Now you've heard the story, you decide who gets the credit. Coincidence or God? You decide." In this sacred space, we are being prepared, as are the Israelite people, for all those moments in our lives when we will have to step to the river's edge and it will be up to us to determine what we see.

Whether we stand at a river and see babies floating by in baskets; or we linger at the crest of a daunting sea where waters miraculously part; or we gaze at the mouth of a blazing furnace where three boys emerge unharmed; or we peer around the door of a rugged stable where a virgin mother gives birth to a son; or we sit on a hillside where five loaves of bread and two fish feed 5,000 people; or we journey out on a raging sea and the storm suddenly calms; or we stand at the entrance of an empty tomb where a stone has been moved away; chances are, there won't be any breaking news bulletins announcing the power and redemptive work of our God. But if we've been to the river, we'll know exactly what we see. If we've been to the river we'll know the footprints of God. We will remember God is never absent from our circumstances but is actively working his plan in our lives.

In 2006, Brazilian news reported the miraculous finding of a two-month-old baby in Pampulha Lake in downtown Belo Horizonte.[7] It was a modern-day Moses story. On the day in question, a park worker is out doing his normal rounds. Something draws him to the edge of the water. Something causes him to notice a black plastic garbage bag floating on a piece of wood. Something captures this man's attention. He hears the sound of a crying baby. Something moves him to be part of a rescue plan. This baby is saved! Coincidence or God? You decide. What do we see when we stand at the river's edge and we choose to look at our world through the lens of faith?

SAMPLE SERMON

THE INTERSECTION OF CULTURE STREET AND GOSPEL BOULEVARD

Text: Ephesians 2:1-10
Dead to Sin Yet Alive in Christ

Focus Statement: Christ calls us to come to terms with what is true about our spiritual condition.

Function Statement: This sermon seeks to open a reflective space where listeners will be inspired to embrace what is true about the life of faith in contrast to what is true about their fallen spiritual condition.

Homiletical Strategy: This sermon seeks to demonstrate how texts from the Epistles can be preached using the orientation/disorientation/re-orientation model. The introduction works to launch the concept of what it means to tell the truth. Strategically this is linked with a humorous personal experience where the preacher receives an e-mail asking whether or not it is true if she is dead!

Moving into **orientation**, the main theme is developed as to how Paul is challenging early believers to come to terms with what is true about their spiritual condition. Here the imagery is created as to how faith and culture collide, and how most people will do what they can to avoid this intersection.

In **disorientation**, primary emphasis is given to what takes place at the corner of Culture Street and Gospel Boulevard. Alternate screenplays are offered as to how Paul could have taken a different approach with the Ephesians, to perhaps be more sensitive or less confrontational. Yet in the end, the harsh reality must stand. We are all dead in our sin and as such become objects of God's wrath.

Moving to **re-orientation**, listeners are challenged to

understand Christ's call to speak not only of what is true of the human condition but also of what is true of the life of faith. Final elements of the sermon invite listeners to complete their journey. Often we hear only the bad news. We switch channels before we hear what is true and life-changing about the Christian experience. Listeners are invited ultimately to decide what is true of their own lived experience.

Introduction:

A few weeks ago, an interesting e-mail popped up on my computer screen. The subject heading asked a question. It said, "Is it true that you are dead?" I have to confess it was one of those moments where I truly wondered what had landed in my in-box. Was it possible someone knew something that I didn't? Yes, it had been an exceptionally busy week. There had been all kinds of unexpected challenges. Yes, I was probably feeling a little worn out. Maybe at least once I might have said, "I feel dead on my feet!" But what was this e-mail all about? Was there something I was missing?

As you would suspect, it was one of those hoax letters telling me I was the beneficiary of a legacy of over $1 million. Since I had not previously written to claim this inheritance, another benefactor had challenged the conditions of the estate. They had gone so far as to forward documents of a bogus funeral service held in my honour. The e-mail went on to say, "We want to confirm whether this is actually true and so we are writing this e-mail address. If we hear nothing from you in two days, we will know that you are dead and we will settle the transfer with the secondary benefactor." If I had been tempted for a minute to think there was any truth in this letter, the large number of spelling and grammar mistakes quickly convinced me otherwise. It was not hard to acknowledge this letter's lack of truth.

Orientation:

Today's text from Ephesians 2:1-10 invites us to think about truth-telling. How do we take the words of a disturbing gospel out into the places where you and I work and live? How does truth-telling happen at the intersection of Culture Street and Gospel Boulevard? What is true of our lives? What is true of the world in which we live? What is true of our spiritual condition and how can we engage conversations that enable us to embrace the truth of the gospel message?

I have a hunch this was the Apostle Paul's challenge as he wrote to the believers in Ephesus. In Ephesians :1, Paul says, "As for you, you were dead in your transgressions and sins, in which you used to live when you followed the ways of this world and of the ruler of the kingdom of the air, the spirit who is now at work in those who are disobedient." If this picture is not dark enough, Paul layers it on again. "In fact," he says, "it's not just about you, but all of us also lived among them at one time, gratifying the cravings of our flesh and following its desires and thoughts. Like the rest, we were by nature deserving of wrath."

We cannot help but feel the weight of Paul's words. Maybe there were those in Ephesus who were sitting up trying to adjust their hearing aids; or there were those that were saying, "Paul, can you just rewind that again for us one more time? Surely, what we heard cannot be right. It cannot be all this bad. Surely, Paul, not everyone is as degraded as you suggest. Life must have some happiness and joy in it. There have to be some good living people in this world for whom this description simply does not apply." Here on the corner of Culture Street and Gospel Boulevard, the truth about our spiritual condition comes before us and slams on its screeching brakes. It swerves into our lane. It lays on the horn and it demands that we pay attention. The truth demands that we talk about the very things that are inhibiting a quality relationship with Jesus Christ.

Disorientation:

As early Christian believers sought to work out the reality of their spiritual condition, so it remains the primary challenge of the Christian Church today. Christ calls us to consider the truth of our spiritual condition to determine whether we are in right relationship with him. Unfortunately, for lots of people, there is total avoidance of the intersection at Culture Street and Gospel Boulevard. Many people purposefully set their GPS to get as far away from the intersection as possible. Some people make their decision to detour; some people take an alternate route; some people drive right on by!

Interestingly for Salvationists, what we are experiencing and what we are observing is not a new challenge. In fact, the Apostle Paul and Catherine Booth, the co-Founder of The Salvation Army, had something in common. It surfaces in an excerpt from a sermon Catherine preached in 1883. She said this: "Satan has got men and women fast asleep in sin and it is his great device to keep them so. We may sing songs about the sweet by and by, preach sermons, say prayers and go the jog trot round and round ... till doomsday and [Satan] will never concern himself about us if we don't wake anybody up." Catherine said, "That is your responsibility, you Christians ... wake them up. Wake them up and remember that sinners are indifferent to the things of Christ."

William Booth went on to say in 1904 at a Staff Officer's Councils how there seemed to be "a great lackadaisical 'take it easy' way of things.... What I plead for [said William] is that in our talking there would be a real declaration of truth, a real attacking of sin and a real urging to the doing of the will of God all the time."

(*Alternate screenplay*) I suppose we could imagine Paul taking a different approach in his letter to the Ephesians. He could have written about weather changes. He could have asked about family. He could have devoted his writing to talk about current economic challenges or even matters of financial management in the Church. But Paul chooses to speak about matters of the heart. He dares to engage the hard conversation: "You were dead in your transgressions and sin; you used to follow the ways of the world and the ruler of the kingdom of the air; you lived satisfying the cravings of the sinful nature and we were all objects of God's wrath. That is where you were (says Paul) but hear this word of truth."

Re-orientation:

Because of his great love for us, God, who is rich in mercy, makes us alive with Christ even when we were dead in transgressions—it is by grace you have been saved. And God raised us up with Christ and seated us with him in the heavenly realm (Ephesians 2:4-6 *NIV*).

While the gospel demands we tell people how dark and how hopeless life is without Jesus Christ, there's a counterpart to be told. We have the privilege of telling people how rich life in Christ can be. **When culture and gospel meet, we not only speak the truth of our spiritual condition. We speak what is true about the life of faith!**

As we look back to our text, see significant insights. Paul wants us to understand the importance of a balanced conversation. When we speak of what is true of the human condition, we give equal emphasis to what is true about of the life of faith. For the gift of God's great love and grace extends to all human beings, regardless of race, colour, creed or situational location. The mercy of God is rich and extravagant. It doesn't matter how distant or removed we may be from the intersection of Culture Street and Gospel Boulevard, God wants us to know the new life that can be ours through Jesus Christ our Lord. God raises us up so that *in the coming ages ... he might show the incomparable riches of his grace expressed in his kindness to us in Christ Jesus.* Paul says, that's the truth. This is the truth about the life of faith! Yes, we are all hopeless, fallen sinners, but see what God has done for you through the cross.

Even though we do not deserve it; even though we are unworthy in every way, God pours out the riches of his grace upon us. Those places in our life wrought with pain, grief and darkness can be alive again by the power of Christ within us. At this intersection of Culture Street and Gospel Boulevard, we preach a faith that is truly worth having.

It is the faith that sustains us when we hear the words "terminal, no hope." It is the foundation upon which we stand when an employer says, "We regret to inform you your services are no longer needed." It is the anchor that holds us when life blows in storms of chaos and confusion. We say, "We have a faith that is worth having!" When we locate ourselves at the centre of Culture Street and Gospel Boulevard, we find ourselves at home in the comfort and mercy of God.

A couple of years ago, I had the opportunity to visit my birthplace in a small remote village in the south of England. We had actually planned all kinds of sights to see on this particular trip. To be honest, I was not sure this tangent to my hometown was really going to be worth it. I was not sure we even had enough information to find what we were looking for. I was only working from limited conversation with my parents and the memory of a five-year-old child. My husband actually had to work quite hard to convince me not to give up the journey. There were no guarantees that the trip was going to be profitable. Yet as we made our way down winding country roads and yes, accidently a couple times into the middle of farmer's fields, eventually I found my home. I found my roots. I found a place of belonging.

Many of us may be tempted to give up our journey toward the intersection of Culture Street and Gospel Boulevard. Some of us may struggle to be convinced the trip is worth it. In reality, we are giving up our journey to the cross where we can find a life and a faith that is truly worth every mile of the way. Thanks to Paul, we already know what is true about our spiritual condition. Praise God! We can also know what is true of the life of faith. In this sacred meeting place, dead things find new life and the eternal inheritance exceeds anything we could ever dream or imagine. Amen.

Chapter 8

DEFINING 21ST-CENTURY "POSTS"

EST THE CONCEPTS "POSTMODERN AND POST-CHRISTIAN" become slippery terms that lack clarity and definition, the following is offered by means of background and contextual explanation.

Postmodernism

As society approached the turn of the millennium and ushered in the 21st century, social commentators were quick to assess the entering of a new phase of history called *postmodernity*. In many respects, it was a signal that the modern era was fading, along with all of the assumptions and value systems that had shaped 20th-century thought. To assist understanding of how this historical reality evolved, Robert Webber, in *Ancient Future Faith*, offers the following seven stages of postmodern development:

> 1870–Prehistory. In 1875, Arnold Toynebee saw Western history as the final phase of a proletariat (industrial working class) civilization.

> 1950–Modernity in decline. The questioning of modern assumptions in science and philosophy.

> 1960–Deconstruction; the countercultural shift. The desire to break away from traditional norms. (The hippie generation comes into its own.)

> 1975–The rise to eclecticism. New respect for minorities,

variety and different lifestyles. Pluralism becomes part of society's working vocabulary.

1979–A new interest in historical memory. A postmodern classicism emerged in art and architecture.

1980–Critical reactions to contemporary culture. The consumer culture and the manipulations of the information age are brought under attack.

1990–The emergence of the postmodern paradigm. Revisionary postmodernism begins to construct a worldview through "a revision of modern premises and traditional concepts."[1]

Recognizing the unrelenting arrival of postmodernism, the task of social commentators was to identify the influence postmodern thought would have on worldview. Conversely, the Church in response seeks to understand the challenges a new worldview brings to present proclamation of Christian faith. Webber offers this concise comparative analysis:

Modern Worldviews said …	Postmodern Worldviews say …
Knowledge is attainable.	Knowledge is not attainable.
Universal truth only based on scientific method.	No universal worldview; all truth is relative.
Optimistic view of humanity.	Recognition of dualism—the conflict between good and evil.
By reason we can find one overarching meta-narrative that speaks about the truth of the world.	The world is full of competing narratives, none of which are universal truth.
Emphasis should be given to individualism.	Community is most important.
Give emphasis to propositional knowledge (facts).	Return to myth, image, metaphor, story, analogy (knowing in community).[2]

As a result of these weighted distinctions, the most significant issue pressing to the surface is how truth is to be understood in a postmodern context. For the postmodern, the argument is represented as clear and decisive; there are no absolutes. Gene Veith, in *Postmodern Times*, cites what becomes most troubling to the Christian Church when this perspective is given merit and credence—society loses a sense of moral consciousness:

While people have always committed sins, they at least acknowledged these were sins. A century ago a person may have committed adultery flagrantly and in defiance of God and man, but he would have admitted that what he was doing was a sin. What we have today is not only immoral behaviour but a loss of moral criteria. This is true even in the Church. We face not only a moral collapse but a collapse in meaning. "There are no absolutes."[3]

While the pull of postmodernity to redefine what constitutes right behaviour and right living cannot be minimized, this tension sits in further conflict with how postmoderns understand the authority of the Church and the path toward salvation that it represents. In this perspective, Veith argues that postmoderns are attacking the Church on new grounds, and in order to minister effectively in a postmodern context, contemporary believers must understand what they are truly up against:

> ... modernists would argue in various ways that Christianity is not true. One hardly hears this objection any more. Today the most common critique is that "Christians think they have the only truth." The claims of Christianity are not denied; they are rejected because they purport to be true. Those who believe "there are no absolutes" will dismiss those who reject relativism as "intolerant," as trying to force their beliefs on people.[4]

In this respect, postmodernity would seem to press an agenda to push the Church into the margins of society. As this happens, the relevance of the Christian message is minimized in its ability to influence the future transformation of the world. Eddie Gibbs, in *Church Next*, argues, "Secular society only allows the Church's representatives back on stage on its own terms. They may serve as therapists, as chaplains of civil religion ... or as celebrants of ceremonial religion. But the secular world allows no place for the prophet or the priest."[5]

The Marriage of Postmodern and
Post-Christian Terminology

Alongside that which has been described as relative to post-modern culture, it is critical to identify the fallout this has had upon the Christian Church and the accompanying conversations that evolved. As consideration was specifically given to the defining influence the Church had on society and vice versa, it was evident some ground had been lost. Recognizing that Christianity had been the "religion of the empire" for almost 1,700 years, dating back to the rule of Constantine (AD 312), slowly it was becoming evident how Christianity might be perceived to be in decline or "pushed in the margins." As identified by Rodney Clapp in *A Peculiar People*, "for the better part of recorded history, the Church [had] become the sponsor of western civilization." As the threads of postmodern thinking have woven their way into the fibre of contemporary society, the result has been a movement of the Christian Church to the peripherals of the world's stage. Strictly speaking, a post-Christian world becomes one where Christianity no longer stands as the dominant civil religion, but a world that has gradually over a period of time assumed values, cultural distinctions and worldviews that are not necessarily Christian. This has not only impacted the numbers of people found in the common pew, but in broader strokes it is evidenced in the way countries have chosen to govern and the laws that have been established. Ultimately, we identify a marriage between postmodern beliefs and post-Christian outcomes.

While one would expect this concept "post-Christian" to be a term launched within the turning of the millennium, interestingly the first usage of the word dates back to the early 1960s. Evidence of this is found when French theologian Gabriel Vahanian argued for the *The Death of God*. His contention was that secular society had lost all sense of the sacred. Bradley Hertel and Hart Nelson, in *Are We Entering a Post-Christian Era?*, went on to acknowledge how this time in history no longer seems to represent uncertainty regarding Christian beliefs but rather outright disbeliefs.[6] This parallels some of the period of deconstruction that Webber previously identified.

While much could be said on this evolution of free thought, what remains is a defining picture of the diminishing place of the Church in secular society; a post-Christian era. Henri Nouwen likens it to a period in which he served as a chaplain on board a cruise liner. One day he stood on the bridge as the ship was making its way through an intensely thick fog. As the captain nervously paced, listening to a radar operator explaining his position between other ships, he collided with the ship's chaplain. Filled with anxiety, the captain cursed the chaplain and told him to stay out of the way. "But," says Nouwen, "when I was ready to run away, filled with feelings of incompetence and guilt, he came back and said: 'Why don't you just stay around? This might be the only time I need you.'" Nouwen went on to explain how the experience is representative of the place in which the Church now seeks to serve. "There was a time when we felt like captains running our own ships, with a great sense of power and self-confidence." Society readily embraced the presence we were offering. But now the fog has rolled in. Society may feel at times we are standing in its way, unless there is some wake of impending crises about to overwhelm. Nouwen concludes that "Christians long to touch the centre of men and women's lives but often find themselves on the peripherals, pleading in vain for admission."[7]

With all of this said, we cannot speak of the challenges of preaching a disturbing gospel without recognizing the realities of our 21st -century context. A marriage has taken place between postmodern thought and post-Christian outcomes. A significant shift has occurred in secular society as the waves of these two entities have washed over the dusty paths the Church has already travelled. It is a new day— theologically, philosophically and morally speaking. Into this reality, the message of a disturbing gospel still must go.

APPENDIX A

THE HOMILETIC OF CHARLES GRANDISON FINNEY (1792-1875)

The following excerpts are offered by means of overview to delineate what was distinct about the revivalistic fervour of Finney's preaching.

All preaching must be understood

Based upon personal experience:

> I sat in the gallery [said Finney] and observed that the parson placed his manuscript in the middle of his Bible, and inserted the four fingers of each hand at the places, where were to be found the passages of Scripture to be quoted, in the reading of the sermon. This made it necessary for him to hold his Bible and rendered all gesticulation with his hands impossible.... I observed that when his fingers were all read out, he was near the close of his sermon. His reading was altogether *unimpassioned and monotonous*. And although the people attended very closely, ... it was not much like that which I thought preaching out to be.[1]

Representing his formative learning as a lawyer:

> When I was at the bar I used to take it for granted when I had a jury of respectable men, that I should have to repeat over my main positions about as many times as there were persons in the jury box. I learned that unless I did so, illustrated, and repeated and turned the main points over—the main points of law and of evidence—then I should

lose my case.... Our object ... is not to make a speech in language; not to display our oratory.... Hence we are set upon being understood.[2]

Keys to being understood:

1. Clearly defined structure
2. Repetition
3. Parallel rhythm of points
4. Conversational language

I [said Finney] have sometimes heard ministers preach, even when there was a revival, when I have wondered what that part of the congregation would do, who had no dictionary. So many phrases were brought in, manifestly to adorn the discourse, rather than to instruct the people, that I have wanted to tell the man, "Sit down and not confound the people's minds with your barbarian preaching, that they cannot understand."[3]

All preaching must be calculated to the human conscience

Appeal to the feelings alone will never convert sinners [said Finney]. If the preacher deals too much in these, he may get up an excitement, and have wave after wave of feeling flow over the congregation, and people may be carried away in the flood with false hopes. The only way to secure sound conversions is to deal faithfully with the conscience. If attention flags at any time, appeal to the feelings again, and rouse it up, but do your *work* with the conscience.[4]

Excerpt from sermon: "The Excuses of Sinners Condemn God"

> You charge that God is unreasonable. The truth is that God is the most reasonable of all beings.... Says that mother—"How can I be religious? I have to take care of my children?" Indeed and can't you get time to serve God? What does God require of you? That you should forsake and neglect your children? No, indeed, he asks you to take care of your children—good care of them; and *do it all for God.*[5]

All preaching should aim for a verdict

Final sermon paragraph of "The Excuses of Sinners Condemn God"

> Remember it is not I who press this claim upon you—but it is God. God himself commands that you repent today—this hour. You know your duty, you know what religion is—what it is to give your heart to God. And now I come to my final question—*Will you do it?* Will you abandon all your excuses, and fall, a self-condemned sinner, before a God of love, and yield to Him yourself—your heart and your whole being, henceforth and forever? *Will you come?*[6]

APPENDIX B

FIRST-TIME SEEKERS
IN THE SALVATION ARMY
A Comparative Analysis from 1980 to 2012

Canada and Bermuda Territory

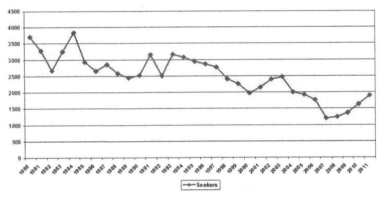

143

APPENDIX C

QUESTIONS FOR FUTURE DISCUSSION

1. How often should preaching attend to the themes of heaven and hell? How does the preacher discern what is truly needed for the ultimate spiritual formation of a congregation?

2. How can preachers best be helped to come to terms with those things that would inhibit their own vibrant proclamation of spiritual truths? What is most needed to excite and energize today's preachers to the preaching task?

3. What would change, homiletically speaking, if hermeneutically preachers were asking more specifically what is disturbing about biblical texts?

4. Recognizing the challenges of the postmodern/post-Christian era, how can the discipline of homiletics further help preachers to step into preaching which truly seems offensive to the contemporary listener?

5. What check points will be necessary to ensure adequate theological substance is informing the assimilation of a Booth homiletic with a new Salvationist homiletic?

6. Given the imprints of others on the lives of William and Catherine Booth, and their subsequent impact on Salvationist preachers, what legacy will today's preachers hand on to those who will follow in their steps? What is the true opportunity of this homiletical moment?

APPENDIX D

FINAL CHECKLIST FOR PREACHING

1. Have I sufficiently orientated myself to the text? Do I grasp the original setting and what is going on in the world to which the text was first directed?

2. Have I investigated the tensions of the text? Do I have a clear picture of what is troubling, ironic or unsettling? Have I identified where the text's speed bumps are?

3. Do I understand why the original writer felt it important to address his audience with the content of the text?

4. Have I isolated what the intended impact of the text was for the text's first audience? (For example, if the text inspires faith, challenges commitment or evokes desire for worship, so should the sermon).

5. Have I considered alternate screenplays? By entertaining what does not happen in the text, what truth about God becomes more obvious?

6. Do I have a clear structure established for my sermon?

7. Have I identified focus and function statements?

8. Is a recurring phrase or sentence, used in the sermon, to assist in anchoring theological claims?

9. Do I move close enough to the lived reality of my listeners? Will listeners see the preacher's own connectedness to their world?

10. Will the sermon say something important about God?

11. Will the sermon contribute anything towards the listener's preparation for eternity?

12. Have I, the preacher, been disturbed by the claims the text makes upon my own life? (Only then am I ready to rise to the pulpit!)

APPENDIX E

RECOMMENDED READING

To explore further models and strategies for preaching a disturbing gospel, consider:

Arthurs, Jeffrey D. *Preaching with Variety*. Grand Rapids: Kregel Publications, 2007.

> Recognizing the ways in which varying biblical genres can stretch a preacher in sermon preparation, Arthurs focuses on defining what a biblical text does and how it communicates. Helpful strategies conclude each chapter that will invite the biblical text to speak through its own voice.

Brueggemann, Walter. *The Militant Word*. Minneapolis: Fortress Press, 2007.

> Emphasizing the need of today's congregants to hear a counter-script to that which the world represents, Brueggemann offers helpful strategies as to how the preacher invites the listener out of his or her context into the biblical world. Guided by specific methodology, Brueggemann assists the preacher in understanding how listeners can find a place of return, where they might re-see and re-describe their circumstances in light of biblical truth.

Edwards, J. Kent. *Deep Preaching*. Nashville: B&H Academic, 2009.

> Pressing the need for preachers to move beyond superficiality in the pulpit, Edwards provides helpful exegetical strategy to assist preachers in strengthening their approach to the pulpit.

Graves, Mike. ed. *What's the Matter with Preaching Today?* Louisville: Westminster John Knox Press, 2004.

A compilation of essays from notable preachers in the field of homiletics addressing Harry Emerson Fosdick's timeless question, "What's the matter with preaching?", published in *Harper's Magazine,* 1928. The challenges of the contemporary pulpit are identified, alongside helpful suggestions for improving the preacher's effectiveness.

Hogan, Lucy Lind. *Graceful Speech.* Louisville: Westminster John Knox Press, 2006.

A helpful preaching primer that gives systematic treatment of the sermonic process with key emphasis toward the preacher becoming a *detective of the divine.*

Montoya, Alex. *Preaching with Passion.* Grand Rapids: Kregel Publications, 2000.

Holding that *preaching is logic on fire,* Montoya unpacks what it means to preach with authority, urgency, compassion, conviction and brokenness. The matter of delivery is emphasized and how passionate biblical preaching will involve the lively engagement of the entire body.

Smith, Robert Jr. *Doctrine that Dances*. Nashville: B&H
Academic, 2008.

Challenging the idea that preachers are often guilty of
serving sermonic snacks instead of the doctrinal meat of
the Word, Smith argues that soft theology will not sustain
believers on the battlefield. Using the extended metaphor
of the preacher as exegetical escort, readers discover
how doctrine can find fresh and vibrant expression in
their preaching and how this can relate to difficult biblical
themes.

Stiller, Brian C. *Preaching Parables to Postmoderns*.
Minneapolis: Fortress Press, 2005.

A very practical resource for the preaching of parables,
which includes treatment of cultural factors impacting the
biblical text; development of how postmodern thinkers
will struggle with the text; the surprise of the parable;
and insights into the text's big idea defined by the
identification of subject and complement.

Wilson, Paul Scott. *Setting Words on Fire*. Nashville: Abingdon
Press, 2008.

Representing the necessity for good teaching to be
foundational to all preaching, Wilson challenges readers to
consider whether true proclamation is being achieved in
their pulpits. According to Wilson, "Teaching is like taking
a bus tour to some royal estate that is wonderful in its own
right, yet what a difference is made if by the journey's end,
one actually meets the owner." Arguing that it is the goal
of every preacher to help people meet God, Wilson offers
helpful strategies for proclaiming varying biblical genres,
including those texts that speak to condemnation, lament
and stern exhortation.

_____. *The Four Pages of the Sermon.* Nashville: Abingdon Press, 1999.

Guided by the themes trouble in the text, trouble in the world, good news in the text and good news in the world, Wilson offers a helpful way for preachers to reshape the structure of their sermons. Using a metaphorical four-page model, the goal of such an approach is that preaching become more attentive to theology while achieving sermons that will readily invite listeners to keep connected beyond the opening scene. Material is organized to address the natural rhythms of a preacher's working week with ample supporting illustrations to assist the reader's journey. Variations on the four-page model are offered in the conclusion.

_____. *Broken Words.* Nashville: Abingdon Press, 2004.

This book reads as an excellent companion to *The Four Pages of the Sermon.* Specific sermon examples are given throughout which provide fresh insight into the four-page model. Readers will discover in practical ways how to navigate difficult texts and themes for preaching.

BIBLIOGRAPHY

A) Sources Relating to the Booth Homiletic

20 Centuries of Great Preaching, Wesley to Finney. Edited by Clyde E. Fant and William M. Pinson. Vol. 3. Waco: Word Books, 1971.

Charles G. Finney: An Autobiography. London: The Salvationist Publishing and Supplies Ltd., n.d.

"Christian Mission Work." *The Christian Mission Magazine* (October 1874), 274-76.

"Flames of Fire—William Bramwell." *The Christian Mission Magazine* (1 October 1870), 149.

"How to Deal with Procrastinating Sinners." *The Officer* (September 1918), 218-20.

"How to Use the Speaking Voice." *The Field Officer* 17, no. 9 (September 1909), 340-43.

"Illustrations and Quotations." *The Officer's Review* 4, no. 2 (March-April 1935), 183-89.

"Importance of Bible Study." *The Field Officer* 15, no. 12 (December 1907), 457-58.

Lectures on Revivals of Religion. Edited by William G. McLoughlin. Cambridge, MA: The Belknap Press of Harvard University Press, 1960.

The Memoirs of Charles G. Finney. Edited by Gath M. Rosell and Richard A.G. Dupuis. Grand Rapids: Zondervan, 1989.

"Original Outlines of Addresses." *The Field Officer* 18, no. 5 (May 1910), 192-93.

"Papers on Soul Winning." *The Officer* (November 1923), 415-17.

"The Power of Direct Personal Attack Upon Sinners." *The Officer* 23, no. 10 (October 1915), 649-56.

"The Preaching That Wins Souls." *The Field Officer* 17, no. 9 (September 1909), 321-23.

"The Salvation Army Officer as Preacher." *The War Cry* (July 27, 1912).

The Salvation Army, Its Origin and Development. rev. ed. London: Salvationist Publishing and Supplies Ltd., 1945.

"Soul Saving Memorials." *The War Cry* (September 7, 1912), 7.

"The Spirit of an Officer." *The Field Officer* 16, no. 9 (September 1908), 321-24.

"Windows into Truth." *The Officer* 36, no. 3 (March 1923), 259-64.

Barnes, Cyril J. *The Founder Speaks Again*. London: Salvationist Publishing and Supplies Ltd., 1960.

Begbie, Harold. *Life of William Booth*. 2 vols. London: MacMillan and Co., Ltd., 1925.

Booth, Bramwell. *Bible Battle-Axes*. London: The Salvationist Publishing and Supplies, Ltd., 1901.

_____. "Catherine Booth: A Chapter of Reminiscences." *The Staff Review* 3, no. 2 (April 1928), 127-36.

_____. "Catherine Booth's Public Ministry." *The Staff Review* 7, no. 4 (October 1927), 380-81.

_____. "How the Buttons Came Off." *The Staff Review* 10 (April 1924).

_____. "The Peril of Formalism." *The Officer* 23, no. 4 (April 1915), 217-23.

Booth, Catherine. *Aggressive Christianity*. London: Simpkin, Marshall, Hamilton, Kent & Co., Ltd., 1880.

_____. *Life and Death*. The Salvation Army, 1883. http://www.gospeltruth.net/booth/cath (accessed January 22, 2007).

_____. *Papers on Aggressive Christianity*. London: International Headquarters, 1880.

_____. *Papers on Godliness*. London: International Headquarters, 1890.

Booth, William. "Old Men, Women, Little Children, Sons of God." *A Record of the Evangelistic Work among the People and Organ of The Christian Mission*. II: (1869-1870).

_____. "The Army and the Bible." *The Field Officer* 7, no. 1 (January 1927), 116-18.

_____. "Consistency." *The Staff Review* 8, no. 1 (January 1928), 114-17.

_____. "Consistency with the Doctrine of Jesus Christ." *The Staff Review* 7, no. 4 (October 1927), 492-500.

_____. "Consistency with the Doctrine of Sin." *The Staff Review* 8, no. 3 (July 1928), 369-70.

————. "Consistency with the Doctrine of the Judgment Day." *The Staff Review* 8, no. 3 (July 1928), 370-73.

————. "Development of Officers." *The Staff Review* (January 1923), 1-10.

————. *The Doctrines of The Salvation Army Prepared for the Training Homes.* London: International Headquarters, 1892.

————. *The General's Messages.* 47 vols. St. Albans: The Salvation Army Printing Works, 1908.

————. "Hints to a Preacher." *East London Christian Mission* I (1868).

————. "Holiness—an Address at the Conference." *The Christian Mission Magazine* (August 1877), 193-98.

————. *How to Preach.* New York: The Salvation Army, 1979.

————. *International Staff Council Addresses.* London: The Salvation Army Book Department, 1904.

————. "A Man Who Pleased God." *The Staff Review* 6, no. 1 (1926), 123-24.

————. "Moses—Leader and Maker of Men." *The Staff Review* 10 (April 1924), 101-12.

————. *Religion for Every Day.* London: The Salvation Army Book Department, 1902.

————. "A Survey of Our Riches." *The Staff Review* 9, no. 2 (May 1929), 232-38.

————. "Talk in Public Meetings." *The Officer* 34, no. 3 (March 1922), 218-23.

————. "The Territorial Commander and the Development of His Officers." *The Staff Review* 6 (April 1923), 93-106.

————. *The General's Letters, 1885.* London: Salvationist Publishing and Supplies Ltd., 1885.

Booth-Tucker, F.L. *The Life of Catherine Booth.* 2 vols. London: International Headquarters, 1892.

Brengle, Samuel Logan. "Problems of the Sunday Night Prayer Meeting." *The Staff Review* 8, no. 2 (April 1928), 196-98.

————. "What of the Army's Present and Future." *The Staff Review* 9, no. 1 (January 1929), 81-85.

Caractacus. *The Question of Questions* London: S. W. Partridge & Co., 1882.

Caughey, James. *Methodism in Earnest.* Richmond: John Early, Methodist Episcopal Church, South, 1852.

Collier, Richard. *The General Next to God.* London: Collins Press, 1965.

Crucible. "Every Officer an Agitator." *The Officer* 24, no. 10 (1916), 805-

808.

Cunningham, Alfred G. "The Staff Officer as a Teacher of Sound Doctrine." *The Staff Review* 6, no. 2 (April 1926) 158-68.

Cuthbert, David. "The Fifty-First Psalm." *The Officer* 34 (February 1922), 135-39.

Garipey, Henry. "Our Heritage—a Retrospective." *The War Cry* (August 5, 1989).

Gibbin, H.E. "Compelling the Attention of the People." *The Officer* 36, no. 3 (March 1923), 218-20.

Green, Roger. *Catherine Booth—A Biography of the Cofounder of The Salvation Army*. Grand Rapids: Baker Books, 1996.

———. *War on Two Fronts*. Atlanta: The Salvation Army Supplies, 1989.

Higgins, E.J. "The Centenary of the Founder." *The Staff Review* 9, no. 2 (May 1929), 143-52.

Jeffries, Charles H. "The William Booth Memorial Training College: Changes in the System of Training." *The Staff Review* 10, no. 4 (October 1930), 312-16.

Kitching, Theodore. "Is Invasion Possible?" *The Officer* 24, no. 5 (May 1916), 294-95.

Larsen, David L. *In the Company of Preachers*. Grand Rapids: Kregal Publications, 1998.

Lawley, John. "The General on the Platform." *The Officer* 24, no. 1 (January 1916), 161-62.

McLoughlin, William G. *Lectures on Revivals of Religion*. Cambridge, MA: The Belknap Press of Harvard University, 1960.

Moyles, R.G. *The Salvation Army and the Public*. Edmonton: AGM Publications, 2000.

Murdoch, Norman H. *Origins of The Salvation Army*. Knoxville: The University Tennessee Press, 1994.

Oliphant, W. Elwin. "Recollections of the Army's Founders." *The Staff Review* 9, no. 1 (1929), 63-67.

Parker, J. Newton. "The Preparation of Subject Outlines." *The Officer* 22, no. 5 (May 1914), 375-77.

Parkhurst, Louise G., ed. *Charles G. Finney, Principles of Holiness*. Minneapolis: Bethany House Publishers, 1984.

Peyron, Albin. "The Officer's Preparation for Public Speaking." *The Officer* 23, no. 10 (October 1915), 733-35.

———. "An Officer's Preparation for Public Speaking." *The Officer* 23, no. 8 (August 1915), 603-605.

Railton, G.S. "About Believing." *The Christian Mission Magazine* (October

1874).

_____. "About Sensationalism." *The Christian Mission Magazine* (July 1874), 175-81.

_____. *The Authoritative Life of General William Booth*. George H. Doran Company, 1912. http://www.gutenberg.org/etext/13958 (accessed January 22, 2007).

_____. "Lessons from the Parable of the Sower." *The Field Officer* 18, no. 9 (September 1910), 358-60.

_____. "Outlines of Sermons: Original." *The Christian Mission Magazine* (November 1874), 316.

Robinson, Haddon. "Charles Grandison Finney." In *Concise Encyclopedia of Preaching*, ed. William Willimon and Richard Lischer, 1:140-141. Louisville: Westminster John Knox Press, 1995.

Sandall, Robert. *The History of The Salvation Army*. Vol. 1. New York: The Salvation Army, 1947.

Satterlee, Allen. *Notable Quotables*. Atlanta: The Salvation Army Supplies, 1985.

Smith, J. Evan. *Booth the Beloved*. London: Oxford University Press, 1949.

_____. "A Private Secretary's View." *The Staff Review* 9, no. 1 (1929), 41-46.

Stead, W.T. *Mrs. Booth of The Salvation Army*. London: James Nesbit and Co., 1900.

Taylor, Bramwell. "Preserving the Difference." *The Staff Review* 6, no. 1 (January, 1926), 113-17.

The Chief of Staff. "The Army's Separateness from Others and Unity within Itself." *The Staff Review* 9, no. 1 (January 1929), 51-62.

The Salvation Army. *The Officer* 21, no. 9 (September 1913).

_____. *The Field Officer* 20, no. 4 (April 1912), 156-57.

_____. "Bring Baby." *The Officer* 23, no. 8 (August 1915), 528.

_____. "Christ's Letters to the Seven Churches of Asia—Their Lessons for Present Day Salvationists." *The Officer* (December 1918).

_____. "A Good Voice for Public Speaking—Can It Be Acquired." *The Officer* (December 1918), 487-92.

    Heritage of Holiness. New York: The Salvation Army, 1977.

_____. "Illustrative Hints and Helps." *The Field Officer* 20, no. 1 (January 1912), 29-31.

_____. *Orders and Regulations for Corps Officers*. London: The Salvation Army, 1948.

_____. *Orders and Regulations for Field Officers*. London: The

Salvationist Publishing and Supplies Ltd., 1922.

_____. *Orders and Regulations for Officers in The Salvation Army.* London: International Headquarters, 1921.

_____. "Original Outlines of Addresses." *The Field Officer* 18, no. 4 (April 1910), 153.

_____. "Outlines for Addresses." *The Field Officer* 21, no. 1 (January 1913).

_____. "Outlines of Addresses." *The Officer* 21, no. 7 (July 1913).

The Salvation Army. "Platform Topics." *The Officer* 36, no. 4 (April 1923), 340-45.

_____. *The Salvation Army Its Origin and Development.* Revised ed. London: Salvationist Publishing and Supplies Ltd., 1945.

_____. "The Salvation Army Officer at Work." *The Field Officer* 16, no. 5 (May 1908), 176-78.

_____. "Seasonal Subject Outlines." *The Field Officer* 17, no. 12 (December 1909), 472-76.

_____. "Seed Thoughts and Illustrations." *The Field Officer* 21, no. 3 (March 1913).

_____. *They Said It—William and Catherine Booth.* London: Salvationist Publishing and Supplies Ltd., 1978.

_____. "The Use of Illustrations on the Platform." *The Officer* 24, no. 10 (November 1916), 778-780.

Torchbearer. "In the Highways and Hedges—Practical Papers on Open Air Work." *The Officer* 24, no. 10 (October 1916), 702-704.

Walker, Pamela J. *Pulling the Devil's Kingdom Down.* Los Angeles: University of California Press, 2001.

Whatmore, Hugh E. "This Changing World of Ours—How Shall We Adapt Ourselves to It?" *The Staff Review* 11 (1931), 316-18.

Whidden, Woodrow W. "Wesley's Theology of Preaching and Its Implications for Worship." *Toronto Journal of Theology* 15, no. 2 (Fall 1999), 183-92.

Wilson, Paul Scott. *A Concise History of Preaching.* Nashville: Abingdon Press, 1992.

B) Sources Relating to the Victorian Context

Religion in Victorian Society. Edited by Richard J. Helmstadter and Paul T. Phillips. London: University Press of America Inc., 1985.

Cody, David. "Evangelicalism." *The Victorian Web* (2008). http://victorianweb.org/religion/evangel1.html (accessed July 2, 2008).

Ensor, R.C.K. *The Oxford History of England 1870-1914.* Edited by G.N. Clark. London: Clarendon Press, 1952.

Green, Roger J. *War on Two Fronts—the Redemptive Theology of William Booth.* Atlanta: The Salvation Army Supplies, 1989.

Heenet, Brian. *A Different Kind of Gentleman.* Hamden, CT: Archon Books, 1976.

Hibbert, Christopher. *The Horizon Book of Daily Life in Victorian England.* New York: American Heritage Publishing Co., Inc., 1975.

Langbaum, Robert. *The Victorian Age.* Edited by Irving Howe. Essays in History and in Social and Literary Criticism. New York: Fawcett World Library, 1967.

Walker, Pamela J. *Pulling the Devil's Kingdom Down.* London: University of California Press, Ltd., 2001.

Woods, Diana. Ed. *The Church and Childhood.* Vol. 31, Studies in Church History. Oxford: Blackwell Publishers, 1994.

C) Sources Relating to Postmodern/Post-Christian Homiletical Challenges

Confident Witness-Changing World: Rediscovering the Gospel in North America. Edited by Craig Van Gelder. Grand Rapids: William B. Eerdmans Publishing Company, 1999.

The Strange New Word of the Gospel. Edited by Carl E. Braaten and Robert W. Jenson. Grand Rapids: William B. Eerdmans Publishing Company, 2002.

What's the Matter with Preaching Today? Edited by Mike Graves. London: Westminster John Knox Press, 2004.

Altrock, Chris. *Preaching to Pluralists.* St Louis: Chalice Press, 2004.

Barna, George. *Evangelism That Works.* Ventura, CA: Regal Books, 1995.

Bonhoeffer, Dietrich. *Meditating on the Word.* Boston: Cowley Publications, 2000.

Brown Taylor, Barbara. *Speaking of Sin.* Boston: Cowley Publications, 2000.

Clapp, Rodney. *A Peculiar People.* Downers Grove, IL: Intervarsity Press, 1996.

Dawn, Marva J. *Unfettered Hope.* Louisville: Westminster John Knox Press, 2003.

Donahue, John R. *The Gospel in Parable.* Philadelphia: Fortress Press, 1988.

Gibbs, Eddie. *Church Next*. Downers Grove, IL: InterVarsity Press, 2000.

Hamilton, Adam. *Unleashing the Word*. Nashville: Abingdon Press, 2003.

Haselden, Kyle. *The Urgency of Preaching*. New York: Harper & Row, 1963.

Honeycutt, Frank G. *Preaching for Adult Conversion and Commitment*. Nashville: Abingdon, 2003.

Hunter, George G. *How to Reach Secular People*. Nashville: Abingdon Press, 1992.

Jantz, Harold. "Competing for Souls." *The Winnipeg Free Press*, Thursday, March 20, 2008.

Johnston, Graham. *Preaching to a Postmodern World*. Grand Rapids: Baker Book House, 2001.

Kolb, Robert. *Speaking the Gospel Today*. St. Louis: Concordia Publishing House, 1995.

Lischer, Richard. *The End of Words. The Language of Reconciliation in a Culture of Violence*. Grand Rapids: William B. Eerdmans Publishing Company, 2005.

Long, Thomas G. "The Distance We Have Traveled: Changing Trends in Preaching." *Reformed Liturgy and Music* 27, no. 1 (Winter 1983).

———. *Preaching and the Literary Forms of the Bible*. Philadelphia: Fortress Press, 1989.

Longhurst, John. "Does Anyone Believe in Sin Anymore?" *The Winnipeg Free Press*, Sunday, May 4, 2008.

Loscalzo, Craig A. *Apologetic Preaching—Proclaiming Christ to a Postmodern World*. Downers Grove: InterVarsity Press, 2000.

Lose, David. *Confessing Jesus Christ—Preaching Christ in a Postmodern World*. Grand Rapids: William B. Eerdmans Publishing Company, 2003.

Lundblad, Barbara K. *Transforming the Stone—Preaching through Resistance to Change*. Nashville: Abingdon Press, 2001.

McLaughlin, Raymond W. *The Ethics of Persuasive Preaching*. Grand Rapids: Baker Book House, 1979.

Posterski, Donald C. *Reinventing Evangelism*. Downers Grove: InterVarsity Press, 1989.

Prokosh, Kevin. "The Sweet Hereafter." *The Winnipeg Free Press*, Sunday, July 6, 2008, D1.

Quicke, Michael J. *360 Degree Preaching*. Grand Rapids: Baker Academic, 2003.

Ricoeur, Paul. "Biblical Hermeneutics," *Semeia* 4 (1975).

Robinson, Anthony B. and Robert W. Wall. *Called to Be Church*. Grand

Rapids: William B. Eerdmans Publishing Company, 2006.

Smith, Robert, and James Earl Massey. *Doctrine that Dances* (Nashville: B&H Academic, 2008)

Swears, Thomas R. *Preaching to Head and Heart.* Nashville: Abingdon, 2000.

Sweet, Leonard. "A New Reformation: Re-Creating Worship for a Postmodern World." In *Experience God in Worship*, ed. Michael D. Warden Loveland, CO: Group Publishing Inc., 2000.

Tisdale, Leonora Tubbs. *Preaching as Local Theology and Folk Art.* Minneapolis: Fortress Press, 1997.

Troeger, Thomas H. *Imagining a Sermon.* Nashville: Abingdon Press, 1990.

Van Harn, Roger E. *Preacher, Can You Hear Us Listening.* Grand Rapids: William B. Eerdmans Publishing Company, 2005.

Veith, Gene Edward. *Postmodern Times.* Wheaton: Crossway Books, 1994.

Walker, Alan. *Evangelistic Preaching.* Grand Rapids: Zondervan, 1988.

Webber, Robert E. *Ancient-Future Faith.* Grand Rapids: Baker Books, 1999.

Willimon, William H. *The Intrusive Word—Preaching to the Unbaptized.* Grand Rapids: William B. Eerdmans Publishing Company, 1994.

Wilson, Paul. *The Practice of Preaching.* Nashville: Abingdon Press, 1995.

Wuthnow, Robert. *After the Baby Boomers.* Princeton: Princeton University Press, 2007.

ENDNOTES

PREFACE

1   Robert Smith, *Doctrine that Dances* (Nashville: B&H Academic, 2008) 104.
2   The Salvation Army, *The Salvation Army Songbook* (Toronto: Canada and Bermuda Territory, 1989).

INTRODUCTION

1   Catherine Booth, "Adaptation of Measures," *Papers on Aggressive Christianity* (London: International Headquarters, 1880), 8.
2   Catherine Booth, *Life and Death* (London: The Salvation Army, 1883) http:www.gospeltruthnet/booth/cath (accessed January 22, 2007), 3.
3   Pamela J. Walker, *Pulling the Devil's Kingdom Down* (Los Angeles: University of California Press, 2001) 3.
4   Note: "Salvationist" meaning persons of either lay or ordained position who have chosen to define their religious affiliation as an active member of The Salvation Army. In this context, people acknowledge acceptance of the doctrines and principles of the Movement and give themselves, as they are able or as they are called, to the mission of kingdom building and serving suffering humanity.
5   Crucible, "Every Officer an Agitator," *The Officer* 24, no. 10 (1916).
6   Note from this point on the homiletic (or preaching approach) of William and Catherine Booth will be referred to as the Booth homiletic.
7   See Chapter 8 for a descriptive overview of what is meant by postmodern/post-Christian context. For discussion purposes, this work argues that preachers are required to address an audience emerging from postmodern influences and ultimately moving into a post-Christian context where Christianity no longer sits centre stage on the societal platform but must share the spotlight with other religious expressions.
8   Eddie Gibbs, *Church Next* (Downers Grove, IL: InterVarsity Press, 2000), 27.
9   Quoted in David L. Larsen, *The Company of Preachers* (Grand Rapids: Kregel Publications, 1998), 14.

CHAPTER 1 RED-HOT PREACHING

1   John Lawley, "The General on the Platform," *The Officer* 24, no. 1 (January 1916), 161.
2   Bramwell Booth, "Catherine Booth's Public Ministry," *The Staff Review* 7, no. 4 (October 1927), 380-81.
3   F.de L. Booth-Tucker, *The Life of Mrs. Booth*, vol.II (London: The Salvation Army International Headquarters, 1892), 50-51.
4   *Ibid.,* 65
5   Roger Green, *Catherine Booth: A Biography of the Cofounder of The Salvation Army* (Grand Rapids: Baker Books, 1996), 62-63. While seminary training was not an option for William, "it was customary for clergy outside of the established church to receive ministerial

training by studying with an experienced minister, learning the trade, as it were under the watchful eye of a senior pastor. So William moved into the house of Dr. Cooke on February 14, 1854.... His apprenticeship began with a view toward ordination in New Connexion Methodism. William was still trying to develop the study habits recommended by Catherine but confessed that he found the academic side of his training difficult and, for him at least, perhaps actually uninspiring.... Into the speculations of philosophy he never entered, and for the laborious study of theology, it is quite certain that he never had any fruitful inclination.... However, he excelled in his preaching for which he had a natural talent and an obvious love."

6   Ibid.; See Chapters 1 and 2 of Roger Green's book for a helpful treatment on this tension, 17-67.

7   Norman H. Murdoch, *Origins of The Salvation Army* (Knoxville: The University of Tennessee Press, 1994), 22.

8   Ibid., 22-23.

9   Bramwell Booth, *The Authoritative Life of General William Booth* (George H. Doran Company, 1912) 8, http://www.gutenberg.org/etext/13958 (accessed January 22, 2007).

10 Murdoch, *Origins of The Salvation Army*, 22.

11 Green, *Catherine Booth, a Biography of the Cofounder of The Salvation Army*, 40.

12 Murdoch, 23.

13 Harold Begbie, *Life of William Booth*, 2 vols. (London: MacMillan and Co., Ltd., 1925), 31.

14 Ibid.

15 Ibid., 32.

16 W.T. Stead, *Mrs. Booth of The Salvation Army* (London: James Nisbet and Co., 1900) 35.

17 Green, *Catherine Booth*, 30.

18 Ibid., 31.

19 Ibid., see 44-67 for details relating to William and Catherine's first meeting, their subsequent courtship, much represented through long-distance correspondence and their subsequent marriage. The primary struggle centres on William's need to determine denominational affiliation in order to engage in full-time ministry.

20 Catherine Booth, *Aggressive Christianity* (London: Simpkin, Marshall, Hamilton, Kent & Co., Ltd., 1880), 4.

21 Note: *The Officer* is a monthly publication of The Salvation Army; at the point of this quotation its primary audience was exclusively Salvation Army officers.

22 Allen Satterlee, *Notable Quotables* (Atlanta: The Salvation Army Supplies, 1985), 160.

23 "The Salvation Army Officer as Preacher," *The War Cry* (July 27, 1912). Note: *The War Cry* was identified historically as The Official Gazette of The Salvation Army; the first English issue in the United Kingdom was December 27, 1879. Subsequently it became a weekly publication.

24 William Booth, "Hints to a Preacher," *East London Christian Mission* I (1868).

25 Booth, *The Doctrines of The Salvation Army Prepared for the Training Homes* (London: The Salvation Army International Headquarters, 1892), 106.

26 *The Field Officer Magazine* was published as a monthly periodical of The Salvation Army from January 1901 to December 1913. Its primary audience were those serving as active officers "on the field" (i.e. as corps officers or pastors) in The Salvation Army. Subsequently in 1914 it became known as *The Officer*.

27 Bramwell Booth, *Bible Battle-Axes* (London: The Salvationist Publishing and Supplies, Ltd., 1901), preface.

28 Booth, *The Doctrines of The Salvation Army Prepared for the Training Homes*, 109.

29 Ibid., 24.

30 Satterlee, *Notable Quotables*, 13.

31 The Salvation Army, *They Said It-William and Catherine Booth* (London: Salvationist Publishing and Supplies Ltd., 1978), 27.

32 Richard Collier, *The General Next To God* (London: Collins Press, 1965), 25.

33 Pamela J. Walker, *Pulling the Devil's Kingdom Down* (Los Angeles: University of California

Press, 2001), 41-42.

34 William Booth, "Old Men, Women, Little Children, Sons of God," *A Record of the Evangelistic Work among the People and Organ of The Christian Mission* II (1869-1870).

35 *The Salvation Army, Its Origin and Development*, rev. ed. (London: Salvationist Publishing and Supplies Ltd., 1945), 8.

36 Green, *Catherine Booth, a Biography of the Cofounder of the Salvation Army*, 156.

37 *Ibid.*, 153.

38 *Ibid.*; see chapter five for a full treatment of Catherine's defense of women preachers. Cf. Walker, *Pulling the Devil's Kingdom Down*, 22-34.

39 Leonora Tubbs Tisdale, *Preaching as Local Theology and Folk Art* (Minneapolis: Fortress Press, 1997), 32-33. Note Tisdale's emphasis: "Our quest is for preaching that is more intentionally contextual in nature, that is, preaching which not only gives serious attention to the interpretation of biblical texts, but also gives serious attention to the interpretation of the congregations and their sociocultural contexts."

40 Harold Begbie, *Life of William Booth*. Vol. 1. (London: MacMillan and Co., Ltd., 1925) 40-41. cf. Murdoch, *Origins of The Salvation Army*, 9. In reference to the charisma of James Caughey, it is stated: "His pulpit presence was commanding; height, keen eyes, and attractive dark features attracted attention. His bell-like voice was unforgettable, and his tone was packed with attention-arresting Irish-American idioms. But his forte was the use of anecdotes and a frank denunciation of sin. He avoided speculative theology. He incited fear with vivid pictures of hell's fury and God's looming judgment, then abruptly shifted to evocations of Christ's mercy and love."

41 Green, *Catherine Booth*, see 86-87. Reference is made to William and Catherine's less formal association with Caughey and the personal interest he took in their work and ministry. "We took tea with Mr. Caughey and Wm had some conversation with him. Then on Wednesday we dined with him where he is staying and enjoyed a rich treat in his society. On Thursday morning he called at Mr. Wilkins and baptized our boy in the presence of a few friends.... He wrote me [Catherine] an inscription for my Bible and took leave of us most affectionately expressing the deepest interest in our future."

42 James Caughey, *Methodism in Earnest* (Richmond: John Early, Methodist Episcopal Church, South, 1852), 20-21, 26. During this period of revival in Britain, records indicate over twenty thousand souls professing faith in Christ and ten thousand professing sanctification.

43 *Ibid.*, 36.

44 Booth, *Aggressive Christianity*, 11.

45 The Salvation Army, *They Said It-William and Catherine Booth*, 58-59. Cf. William Booth, *Religion for Every Day* (London: The Salvation Army Book Department, 1902) 162. "Publish the salvation of the Bible wherever you go–in the streets–in the barracks–in your home–at your work–everywhere tell the glad tidings ... do not let the Bible rise up in judgment against you, as it surely will, you will either neglect it, or if reading and knowing about the salvation and victory of which it tells, you do not enjoy that salvation and experience that victory."

46 See Appendix A.

47 William G. McLoughlin, *Lectures on Revivals of Religion* (Cambridge, MA: The Belknap Press of Harvard University, 1960), 215-16.

48 For further treatment on the homiletic of Charles Finney, see Appendix A.

49 Murdoch, *Origins of The Salvation Army*, 16.

50 Walker, *Pulling the Devil's Kingdom Down*, 23.

51 See Green, *Catherine Booth*, 125-40.

52 *Ibid.*, 126.

53 Murdoch, *Origins of The Salvation Army*, 17-18.

54 *Ibid.*, 18.

55 Cyril J. Barnes, *The Founder Speaks Again* (London: Salvationist Publishing and Supplies Ltd., 1960), 45.

56 The Salvation Army, *Orders and Regulations for Officers in The Salvation Army* (London: International Headquarters, 1921), 291.

57   See Murdoch, *Origins of The Salvation Army*, 31. This two-step process of salvation was also fully endorsed by mid-19th-century American Revivalism. Influences within the Booths' context stood in full agreement on these issues of doctrinal distinction.

58   *Ibid.*

59   Roger Green, *War on Two Fronts* (Atlanta: The Salvation Army Supplies, 1989), 38. See additional notes, 112-113. "... at Gateshead too, William and Catherine Booth decided that it was incumbent upon them to set forth definitely and regularly the doctrine of full salvation. With John Wesley they had come to the conclusion that the very object of the Atonement was the conquest and removal of indwelling evil, and that the heart could be purified from its evil tendencies which would otherwise prove too strong for it and render it the helpless prey of every passing temptation."

60   Catherine Booth, *Papers on Godliness* (London: International Headquarters, 1890).

61   The Salvation Army, *Heritage of Holiness* (New York: The Salvation Army, 1977), 12.

62   Green, *War on Two Fronts*, 38-39.

63   *Ibid.* Cf. William Booth, "Holiness: An Address at the Conference," *The Christian Mission Magazine* (August 1877).

CHAPTER 2 KEEPING EARLY PULPIT FIRES BURNING

1   R.G. Moyles, *The Salvation Army and the Public* (Edmonton: AGM Publications, 2000) 6. Cf. Elijah Cadman www1.salvationarmy.org.uk/uki (accessed March 30, 2007). Significant background material provided about Cadman, including his innovation of The Salvation Army uniform: "I would like to wear a suit of clothes that would let everyone know that I meant war to the teeth and salvation for the world."

2   *Ibid.*

3   William Booth, *International Staff Council Addresses* (London: The Salvation Army Book Department, 1904), 144.

4   *Ibid.,* 122.

5   *Ibid.,* 124.

6   Theodore Kitching, "Is Invasion Possible?," *The Officer* 24, no. 5 (May 1916), 295.

7   William Booth, "Talk in Public Meetings," *The Officer* 34, no. 3 (March 1922), 219.

8   The Salvation Army, "Outlines for Addresses," *The Field Officer* 21, no. 1 (January 1913), 49. Cf. Bramwell Taylor, "Preserving the Difference," *The Staff Review* 6, no. 1 (January 1926), 113-17. Representing early convictions about The Salvation Army, Brigadier Bramwell Taylor presents a compelling argument as to why Salvationists should be encouraged to preserve the difference of our Movement. "We are separate from the world and a distinctly separate force in the realm of religion ... we are an Army, not a church ... the idea of sermons being preached from our platform is quite incongruous.... Our term is 'songs' not 'hymns.' "

9   *Ibid,* c.f 113-17.

10   J. Evan Smith, *Booth the Beloved* (London: Oxford University Press, 1949), 92-93.

11   "The Preaching that Wins Souls," *The Field Officer* 17, no. 9 (September 1909), 321-23.

12   Caractacus, *The Question of Questions* (London: S. W. Partridge & Co., 1882), 37-38.

13   The Salvation Army, "Christ's Letters to the Seven Churches of Asia—Their Lessons for Present Day Salvationists," *The Officer* (December 1918), 464.

14   The Salvation Army, "Bring Baby," *The Officer* 23, no. 8 (August 1915) 528.

15   The Salvation Army, *Orders and Regulations for Field Officers*, ed. The Salvation Army (London: The Salvationist Publishing and Supplies Ltd., 1922), 108-09.

16   Moyles, *The Salvation Army and the Public*, 178.

17   Penitent form: in both indoor and open-air context, Salvationists would create a place for penitent sinners to come and kneel in public confession of faith, in response to the message proclaimed. Many early converts to The Salvation Army began their journey of salvation kneeling at the side of a simple bass drum.

18   "Christian Mission Work," *The Christian Mission Magazine* (October 1874), 274.

19   *Ibid.,* 276.

20   Note William Booth's life span, 1829-1912.

21   Henry Garipey, "Our Heritage-a Retrospective," *The War Cry* (August 5, 1989), 4-11.

22   E.J. Higgins, "The Centenary of the Founder," *The Staff Review* 9, no. 2 (May 1929), 151.

23   *Ibid.*, 154

24   Roger Green, *Catherine Booth: A Biography of the Cofounder of The Salvation Army* (Grand Rapids: Baker Books, 1996), 283.

25   "Soul Saving Memorials," *The War Cry* (September 7, 1912), 7.

26   Cf. Introduction and Chapter 1.

CHAPTER 3 VICTORIAN ENGLAND WARMS UP TO THE GOSPEL

1   Roger J. Green, *War on Two Fronts—the Redemptive Theology of William Booth* (Atlanta: The Salvation Army Supplies, 1989), 1-8. For full commentary on the Victorian England of William Booth see Green's cited introductory material.

2   Christopher Hibbert, *The Horizon Book of Daily Life in Victorian England* (New York: American Heritage Publishing Co., Inc., 1975), 76. One of the worst abuses was the masters' habit of forcing workers to buy their food and other necessities at shops owned by them or by their relations or friends where prices were inflated. "They tell their men or at least it is understood, 'if you don't buy my groceries, we will not buy your nails.' "

3   *Ibid.*, 113. In 1885, it was estimated that there were as many as 60,000 prostitutes in London. Gentlemen paid especially large sums for little virgins; those under 13 years.

4   *Ibid.*, 68. In describing actual living conditions in London, Hibbert cites: "London was as bad as anywhere ... where low houses, poor streets of brick under red-tiled roofs cross each other in every direction.... It is in these localities that families have been discovered with no other bed than a heap of soot ... sometimes the single room wherein they all huddled in the foul air... a den in which to sleep and die."

5   Robert Langbaum, *The Victorian Age*, ed. Irving Howe, Essays in History and in Social and Literary Criticism (New York: Fawcett World Library, 1967), 64.

6   *Religion in Victorian Society*, ed. Richard J. Helmstadter and Paul T. Phillips (London: University Press of America Inc., 1985), see Preface.

7   R.C.K. Ensor, *The Oxford History of England 1870-1914*, ed. G.N. Clark (London: Clarendon Press, 1952), 137.

8   Hibbert, *The Horizon Book of Daily Life in Victorian England*, 115.

9   *Ibid.*, 118.

10   *Ibid.*, 120.

11   Ensor, *The Oxford History of England 1870-1914*, 140.

12   *Ibid.*, 139.

13   *Religion in Victorian Society*, xiii.

14   Brian Heenet, *A Different Kind of Gentleman* (Hamden, CT: Archon Books, 1976), 11.

15   Hibbert, *The Horizon Book of Daily Life in Victorian England*, 113.

16   Paul Wilson, *The Practice of Preaching* (Nashville: Abingdon Press, 1995), 206-07.

17   David Cody, "Evangelicalism," *The Victorian Web* (2008) 1-2, http://victorianweb.org/religion/evangel1.html (accessed July 2, 2008). For further related references, see materials cited.

18   Ensor, *The Oxford History of England 1870-1914*, 138.

19   Green, *War on Two Fronts—the Redemptive Theology of William Booth*, 2.

20   *Religion in Victorian Society*, 211.

21   Pamela J. Walker, *Pulling the Devil's Kingdom Down* (Los Angeles: University of California Press, 2001), 57.

22   *Ibid.*, 58.

CHAPTER 4 POSTMODERNISTS COOL TO THE GOSPEL

1   Restating previous observations. Victorian England shares with a postmodern/post-Christian context: 1) The ongoing struggle of sin's presence in the world; 2) The disparity of social classes with special sensitivity toward the overwhelming plight of the poor; 3) a sense of individualism; everyone out to achieve for himself/herself.

2   Chris Altrock, *Preaching to Pluralists* (St Louis: Chalice Press, 2004), 8. For the purposes of

this discussion, Altrock defines the postmodern era as that which could also be called post-Christian or anti-Christian. The Boomers (born 1946-1964), Busters (born 1965-1979), and Net-gens (born 1980-early 2000s) are the transitional generation within this cultural shift.

3   *Ibid.*, 9.

4   Note: The phrase *Postmodern Pilgrim* was coined by Leonard Sweet in *Post-Modern Pilgrims* (Nashville: Broadman & Hollman Publishers, 2000), xvii.

5   Richard Lischer, *The End of Words*, The Language of Reconciliation in a Culture of Violence (Grand Rapids: William B. Eerdmans, 2005), 13.

6   George Barna, *Evangelism That Works* (Ventura, CA: Regal Books, 1995), 36.

7   Graham Johnston, *Preaching to a Postmodern World* (Grand Rapids: Baker Book House, 2001), 14.

8   Altrock, *Preaching to Pluralists*, 9.

9   *Ibid.*, 60.

10 Kevin Prokosh, "The Sweet Hereafter," *The Winnipeg Free Press*, Sunday, July 6, 2008, D1. Browne was further cited by this author as misinterpreting a case of a missing 11-year-old boy, suggesting to his parents that he was dead. Four years after this pronouncement, he was found living with his abductor.

11 Altrock, *Preaching to Pluralists*, 61.

12 Ian J. Carr, "My Post-Christian Testimony," (2010), http://www.infidels.org/library/modern/testimonials/carr.html (accessed October 22, 2010).

13 Altrock, *Preaching to Pluralists*, 10.

14 cf. Prokosh, "The Sweet Hereafter." Note within the psychic summary the primacy of Prokosh's message regarding a potential return to life here on earth: "You go with your (spirit) guide to a large temple and view your life and then you decide whether you are going to come back or not."

15 Anthony B. and Robert W. Wall Robinson, *Called to Be Church* (Grand Rapids: William B. Eerdmans Publishing Company, 2006), 224.

16 *Ibid.*

17 George G. Hunter, *How to Reach Secular People* (Nashville: Abingdon Press, 1992), 52.

18 *Ibid.*, 46.

19 Barbara Brown Taylor quoted by Frank G. Honeycutt, *Preaching for Adult Conversion and Commitment* (Nashville: Abingdon, 2003), 78.

20 Donald C. Posterski, *Reinventing Evangelism* (Downers Grove, IL: InterVarsity Press, 1989), 80.

21 Barna, *Evangelism That Works*, 51.

22 *Ibid.*, 56.

23 Robert Wuthnow, *After the Baby Boomers* (Princeton: Princeton University Press, 2007), 42.

24 Cf. William G. McLoughlin, Lectures on Revivals of Religion (Cambridge, MA: The Belknap Press of Harvard University, 1960). "Ministers should never rest satisfied until they have ANNIHILATED every excuse of sinners.... Tear away the last LIE ... and make him feel that he is absolutely condemned before God." Cf. pages 3, 25 of this work.

CHAPTER 5 REKINDLING THE FLAME

1   Michael J. Quicke, *360 Degree Preaching* (Grand Rapids: Baker Academic, 2003), 61.

2   Catherine Booth, "Adaptation of Measures," In *Aggressive Christianity*, ed. International Headquarters. (London: The Salvation Army, 1880), 8.

3   Note: From this point forward the assimilation and re-contextualization of the history and homiletic previously explored will transition from the Booth homiletic to the identity of a new Salvationist homiletic.

4   Note: *The Staff Review* was a quarterly periodical for staff (senior leaders) of The Salvation Army. Vol. 1 was published first in 1922 until 1931. This was a publication intended for private circulation only.

5   William Booth, "Moses—Leader and Maker of Men," *The Staff Review* 10 (April 1924), 103.

6   Catherine Booth, "Adaptation of Measures," 8.

7   David Lose, *Confessing Jesus Christ—Preaching Christ in a Postmodern World* (Grand Rapids: William B. Eerdmans Publishing Company, 2003), 212.

8   Quicke, 36.

9   *Ibid.*, 27.

10   *Ibid.*

11   *Ibid.*

12   Anthony B. and Robert W. Wall Robinson, *Called to Be Church* (Grand Rapids: William B. Eerdmans Publishing Company, 2006) 274.

13   See Chapter 7 for a sample sermon which works to exemplify the principle of enlivening a biblical text by putting it in conversation with modern images and nuances.

14   Marva J. Dawn, *Unfettered Hope* (London: Westminster John Knox Press, 2003), 162. Cf. p. 159. Helpful insights offered as to how the use of language and speech will assist the preacher in reframing new realities for postmodern/post-Christian listeners. "Society perpetuates the reduction of word meanings and thus constantly reduces things, people and God. Over-inflated words do not carry wonder—they attempt to advertise. True words simply convey genuine reality; thus, when we speak of God, our speech should always become tinged with amazement, a sense of both intimate immanence and mysterious transcendence."

15   Eddie Gibbs, *Church Next* (Downers Grove, IL: InterVarsity Press, 2000), 195.

16   *Ibid.*, 196.

17   Adam Hamilton, *Unleashing the Word* (Nashville: Abingdon Press, 2003), 121. cf. 122: "At the end of the day, I believe that is what effective prophetic preaching is supposed to actually do: to actually affect the people who most need to hear it. It is meant to move them to change—to reconsider their life or their views. If you can with humility, respect and great love, offer a challenging word, you have the incredible potential of actually changing the hearts and minds of your listeners." Cf. David Lose, *Confessing Jesus Christ-Preaching Christ in a Postmodern World*, 205.

18   Lose, 124.

19   William H. Willimon, *The Intrusive Word—Preaching to the Unbaptized* (Grand Rapids: William B. Eerdmans, 1994), 60.

20   Barbara K. Lundblad, *Transforming the Stone—Preaching through Resistance to Change* (Nashville: Abingdon Press, 2001), 29.

21   See Appendix B. Recent statistics in The Salvation Army Canada and Bermuda Territory point to a notable decline in first-time seekers using Salvation Army mercy seats or altars. From 1980 through to 2007, a steady decline of 68 percent is noted. While some marginal increases follow, further study is merited to determine what factors have impacted both the fall and the increase in these statistics. (Information provided by The Salvation Army Canada and Bermuda Territorial Headquarters.)

22   Mercy seat: in Hebrew meaning "atonement place." Salvationists draw from the imagery of the Old Testament to give definition to a wooden bench that sits at the front of the sanctuary, otherwise known as an altar for prayer and commitment. In earlier historical context, Salvationists borrowed from the evangelistic practices of Charles Finney, who would invite sinners to the anxious seat. In subsequent years, Salvationists named this the penitent form, where sinners could receive mercy and saints could receive sanctification. More contemporary contexts would reference the mercy seat simply as "a place of prayer."

23   As a point of example, congregants at a Good Friday service might be invited to come and take a nail and hammer it into a make-shift cross, as a symbol of their ownership in the sufferings of Christ. Following a sermon on the woman at the well (John 4), congregants might be invited as a symbol of their own acceptance of living water to come and drink from a punch fountain at the front of the sanctuary. Subsequent to the preaching of the miraculous catch of fish, congregants might write on slips of paper their own needs and concerns, placing them in a fishing net draped across the altar. In so doing, they are publicly affirming the capacity of God to give more than they could ever ask or imagine.

24   Theodore Kitching, "Is Invasion Possible?," *The Officer* 24, no. 5 (May 1916), 294-95. (See also Chapter 2 of this book.)

25   Chris Altrock, *Preaching to Pluralists* (St Louis: Chalice Press, 2004), 11. cf. 127 Altrock calls for a rethinking of how preaching language is used—that it not only convince the mind but

inflame the soul. E.g. Psalm 42:1 "As the deer longs for flowing streams, so my soul longs for you, O God."

26   Richard Lischer, *The End of Words*, The Language of Reconciliation in a Culture of Violence (Grand Rapids: William B. Eerdmans, 2005), 12. Cf.132 "Why should we persist in speaking the gospel in the midst of the assembly? The answer in short is that Jesus sent his followers into the world to speak his message.... For busy pastors the reasons for preaching are hazy at best. It is as if we have been occupied so long with capturing culture's attention that once we have it we have forgotten what we are supposed to say."

27   Barbara Brown Taylor, *Speaking of Sin* (Boston: Cowley Publications, 2000), 3.

28   *Ibid.*, 5-6.

29   See Chapter 7—a sermon sample which highlights the need for both judgment and grace themes to be heard in order that there is validation to the truth of God's promises.

30   Brown Taylor, *Speaking of Sin*, 67.

31   John Longhurst, "Does Anyone Believe in Sin Anymore?," *The Winnipeg Free Press*, Sunday May 4, 2008, B7.

32   Brown Taylor, 83.

33   *Ibid.*, 96.

34   cf. Chapter 1.

35   Altrock, *Preaching to Pluralists*, 135.

36   Gibbs, *Church Next*, 197.

37   Robinson, *Called to Be Church*, 68-69.

38   Leonard Sweet, "A New Reformation: Recreating Worship for a Postmodern World," *Experience God in Worship* (Loveland, CO: Group Publishing Inc., 2000) 182.

39   Aristotle (384-322 BC) was a Greek philosopher, particularly cited in this work due to his emphasis on the place of rhetoric as a means toward persuasive communication. This included three primary elements: logos (the spoken word, does the message make sense to the listener,) pathos (speaking to the emotional state of the audience) and ethos (speaking to demonstrate interest in the audience's welfare.) Cf. G.G. Hunter, 22.

40   Leonora Tubbs Tisdale, *Preaching as Local Theology and Folk Art* (Minneapolis: Fortress Press, 1997), 42.

41   Craig A Loscalzo, *Apologetic Preaching—Proclaiming Christ to a Postmodern World* (Downers Grove, IL: InterVarsity Press, 2000), 36. cf. 40; Emphasis given to postmodern preaching that does not bombard with theological truth, but rather is sensitive to postmoderns' appreciation of stories and takes seriously their desire to be led.

42   "Soul Saving Memorials," *The War Cry* (September 7, 1912), 7.

43   Cf. Chapter 4.

44   Cf. Chapter 1.

45   Quicke, 30. Quoting Long further, "When the voltage drops in the Bible, preachers desperately plug the sermon into any outlet that promises a jolt of energy: psychotherapy, narrative, image, communication theory, personal disclosure and the list goes on. This plunge in scriptural voltage has disabled much of contemporary preaching."

46   *Ibid.*, 115.

47   Dietrich Bonhoeffer, *Meditating on the Word* (Boston: Cowley Publications, 2000), 50-51. Pressing his point further, Bonhoeffer argued that "we must practice our communication with God, otherwise we will not find the right tone, the right word, the right language, when God surprises us with his presence. We must learn the language of God, carefully learn it, work hard at it so we will be able to speak to him.

48   Note at this point that a new term is introduced to this discussion; *a new Salvationist homiletic* is intended to represent the marriage between a Victorian/postmodern approach to preaching, focusing toward the integration of characteristics defining of the Booth homiletic.

49   Thomas G. Long, "The Distance We Have Traveled: Changing Trends in Preaching," *Reformed Liturgy and Music 27*, no. 1 (Winter 1983), 14.

CHAPTER 6 RETURNING TO OUR PLACE OF BEGINNING

1   Cf. Chapter 3.

2   *Ibid.*

3   *Ibid.*

4   *Ibid.*

5   *Ibid.*

6   William Booth, "Hints to a Preacher," *East London Christian Mission* I (1868), 135.

7   See Appendix C for questions emerging from this work which invite future homiletical conversation.

CHAPTER 7 HOW TO PREACH A DISTURBING GOSPEL

1   John R. Donahue, *The Gospel in Parable* (Philadelphia: Fortress Press, 1988).

2   Paul Ricoeur, "Biblical Hermeneutics," *Semeia* 4 (1975), 130

3   *Ibid.*, 118.

4   Thomas Troeger, *Imagining a Sermon* (Nashville: Abingdon Press, 1990), 53

5   Thomas Long, *Preaching and the Literary Forms of the Bible* (Philadelphia: Fortress Press, 1989), 26.

6   _____. *The Witness of Preaching*, 2nd Ed. (Louisville: Westminster John Knox Press, 2005), 108-109. For further discussion, see Chapter 4.

7   "Baby Found in Bag in Brazil Lake" BBC.com (January 29, 2006). http://news.bbc.co.uk/1/hi/world/americas/4659568 (accessed online May 30, 2006).

CHAPTER 8 DEFINING 21ST-CENTURY "POSTS"

1   Robert E. Webber, *Ancient-Future Faith* (Grand Rapids: Baker Books, 1999), 35. Note summary is an adaptation from Charles Jencks, ed., *A Post-Modern Agenda* (New York: St. Martin's, 1992), 10-39.

2   *Ibid.*, 37.

3   Gene Edward Veith, *Postmodern Times* (Wheaton: Crossway Books, 1994), 18.

4   *Ibid.*, 19-20.

5   Eddie Gibbs, *Church Next* (Downers Grove, IL: InterVarsity Press, 2000), 26.

6   Bradley R Hertel, Nelsen, Hart M., "Are We Entering a Post-Christian Era? Relgious Belief and Attendance in America, 1957-1968," *Journal for the Scientific Study of Religion* 13, no. 4 (1974), 409-10.

7   Rodney Clapp, *A Peculiar People* (Downers Grove, Illinois: InterVarsity Press, 1996), 16-17.

APPENDIX A: THE HOMILETIC OF CHARLES GRANDISON FINNEY

1   *The Memoirs of Charles G. Finney*, ed. Gath M. Rosell and Richard A.G. Dupuis (Grand Rapids: Zondervan, 1989), 8-9.

2   *Charles G. Finney—An Autobiography*, (London: The Salvationist Publishing and Supplies Ltd., n.d.), 68-69.

3   *Lectures on Revivals of Religion*, ed. William G. McLoughlin (Cambridge: The Belknap Press of Harvard University Press, 1960), 209.

4   *Ibid.*, 214.

5   *20 Centuries of Great Preaching, Wesley to Finney*, ed. Clyde E. Fant and William M. Pinson, vol.3 (Waco, Texas: Word Books, 1971), 345.

6   *Ibid.*, 360.